HUMANITARIAN LAW VIOLATIONS
IN KOSOVO

Human Rights Watch
New York · Washington · London · Brussels

ISBN: 1-56432-194-0
Library of Congress Catalog Card Number: 98-88735
Cover photograph © Peter Bouckaert/Human Rights Watch

Addresses for Human Rights Watch:
350 Fifth Avenue, 34th Floor, New York, NY 10118-3299
Tel: (212) 290-4700, Fax: (212) 736-1300, E-mail: hrwnyc@hrw.org

1522 K Street, NW, #910, Washington, DC 20005-1202
Tel: (202) 371-6592, Fax: (202) 371-0124, E-mail: hrwdc@hrw.org

33 Islington High Street, N1 9LH London, UK
Tel: (171) 713-1995, Fax: (171) 713-1800, E-mail: hrwatchuk@gn.apc.org

15 Rue Van Campenhout, 1000 Brussels, Belgium
Tel: (2) 732-2009, Fax: (2) 732-0471, E-mail: hrwatcheu@gn.apc.org

Web Site Address: http://www.hrw.org
Gopher Address://gopher.humanrights.org:5000/11/int/Human Rights Watch
Listserv Address: To subscribe to the list, send an e-mail message to
majordomo@igc.apc.org with "subscribe Human Rights Watch-news" in the body
of the message (leave the subject blank).

HUMAN RIGHTS WATCH

Human Rights Watch conducts regular, systematic investigations of human rights abuses in some seventy countries around the world. Our reputation for timely, reliable disclosures has made us an essential source of information for those concerned with human rights. We address the human rights practices of governments of all political stripes, of all geopolitical alignments, and of all ethnic and religious persuasions. Human Rights Watch defends freedom of thought and expression, due process and equal protection of the law, and a vigorous civil society; we document and denounce murders, disappearances, torture, arbitrary imprisonment, discrimination, and other abuses of internationally recognized human rights. Our goal is to hold governments accountable if they transgress the rights of their people.

Human Rights Watch began in 1978 with the founding of its Europe and Central Asia division (then known as Helsinki Watch). Today, it also includes divisions covering Africa, the Americas, Asia, and the Middle East. In addition, it includes three thematic divisions on arms, children's rights, and women's rights. It maintains offices in New York, Washington, Los Angeles, London, Brussels, Moscow, Dushanbe, Rio de Janeiro, and Hong Kong. Human Rights Watch is an independent, nongovernmental organization, supported by contributions from private individuals and foundations worldwide. It accepts no government funds, directly or indirectly.

The staff includes Kenneth Roth, executive director; Michele Alexander, development director; Reed Brody, advocacy director; Carroll Bogert, communications director; Cynthia Brown, program director; Barbara Guglielmo, finance and administration director; Jeri Laber special advisor; Lotte Leicht, Brussels office director; Patrick Minges, publications director; Susan Osnos, associate director; Jemera Rone, counsel; Wilder Tayler, general counsel; and Joanna Weschler, United Nations representative. Jonathan Fanton is the chair of the board. Robert L. Bernstein is the founding chair.

The regional directors of Human Rights Watch are Peter Takirambudde, Africa; José Miguel Vivanco, Americas; Sidney Jones, Asia; Holly Cartner, Europe and Central Asia; and Hanny Megally, Middle East and North Africa. The thematic division directors are Joost R. Hiltermann, arms; Lois Whitman, children's; and Regan Ralph, women's.

The members of the board of directors are Jonathan Fanton, chair; Lisa Anderson, Robert L. Bernstein, William Carmichael, Dorothy Cullman, Gina Despres, Irene Diamond, Adrian W. DeWind, Fiona Druckenmiller, Edith Everett, James C. Goodale, Vartan Gregorian, Alice H. Henkin, Stephen L. Kass, Marina Pinto Kaufman, Bruce Klatsky, Harold Hongju Koh, Alexander MacGregor, Josh Mailman, Samuel K. Murumba, Andrew Nathan, Jane Olson, Peter Osnos, Kathleen Peratis, Bruce Rabb, Sigrid Rausing, Anita Roddick, Orville Schell, Sid Sheinberg, Gary G. Sick, Malcolm Smith, Domna Stanton, and Maya Wiley. Robert L. Bernstein is the founding chair of Human Rights Watch.

ACKNOWLEDGMENTS

This report is based on research conducted in Kosovo, Montenegro, and Albania between May and September 1998. The report was written by Fred Abrahams, researcher, Human Rights Watch and edited by Mike McClintock, deputy program director of Human Rights Watch, and Holly Cartner, executive director, Europe and Central Asia division of Human Rights Watch. Parts were written by Elizabeth Andersen, advocacy director. Additional research was conducted by Peter Bouckaert, Sahr MuhammedAlly, Suzanne Nossel, and Meghan Redmond. Invaluable production assistance was provided by Alex Frangos, Alexandra Perina, and Emily Shaw, associates, Human Rights Watch.

Human Rights Watch would like to acknowledge and thank the many individuals whose contributions made this report possible, especially the human rights groups that are working in Yugoslavia under difficult conditions. Special thanks go to the victims and witnesses of abuses in Kosovo who provided testimony and information in the hope that the perpetrators of war crimes will be brought to justice.

CONTENTS

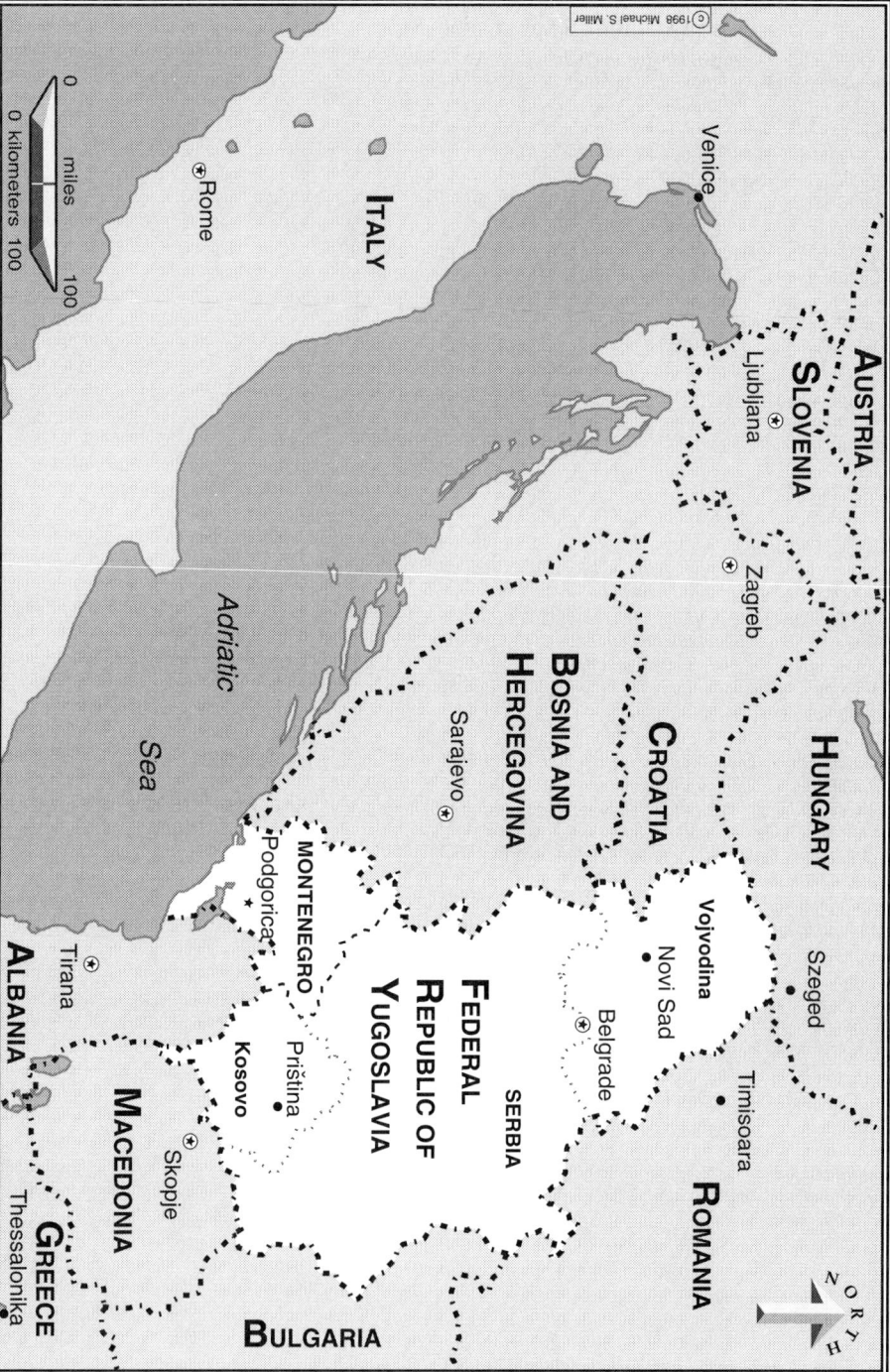

Yugoslavia

© 1998 Michael S. Miller

0 miles 100
0 kilometers 100

ITALY

Rome

Venice

Adriatic

Sea

AUSTRIA

SLOVENIA
Ljubljana

Zagreb

CROATIA

BOSNIA AND HERCEGOVINA
Sarajevo

HUNGARY

Szeged

ROMANIA

Timisoara

MONTENEGRO
Podgorica

FEDERAL REPUBLIC OF YUGOSLAVIA

SERBIA

Vojvodina
Novi Sad

Belgrade

ALBANIA
Tirana

MACEDONIA
Skopje

Kosovo
Priština

GREECE
Thessalonika

BULGARIA

NORTH

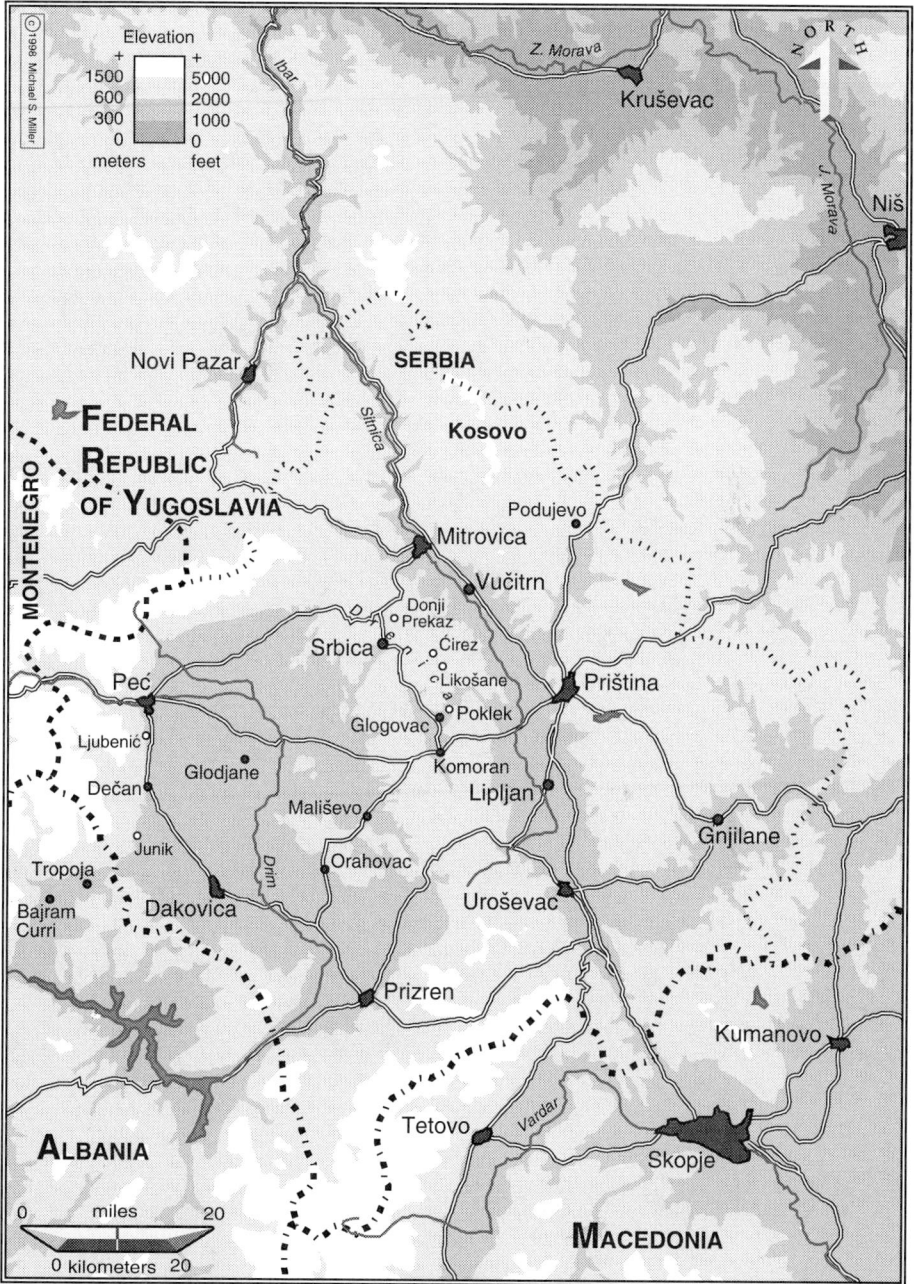

Elevation

meters	feet
1500	5000
600	2000
300	1000
0	0

© 1998 Michael S. Miller

NORTH

Ibar

Z. Morava

Kruševac

J. Morava

Niš

Novi Pazar

SERBIA

Kosovo

Sitnica

FEDERAL REPUBLIC OF YUGOSLAVIA

MONTENEGRO

Podujevo

Mitrovica

Vučitrn

Donji Prekaz

Srbica

Ćirez

Likošane

Priština

Peć

Poklek

Glogovac

Ljubenić

Komoran

Glodjane

Lipljan

Dečan

Mališevo

Gnjilane

Drim

Junik

Orahovac

Tropoja

Uroševac

Bajram Curri

Dakovica

Prizren

Kumanovo

ALBANIA

Tetovo

Vardar

Skopje

MACEDONIA

0 miles 20

0 kilometers 20

Kosovo

1. SUMMARY

This report documents serious breaches of international humanitarian law, the rules of war, committed in Kosovo from February to early September 1998. Future Human Rights Watch reports will provide evidence about atrocities in villages such as Donje Obrinje, Golubovac, and Vranić, the details of which were emerging as this report went to press. (*See* appendices A, B and C). The vast majority of these abuses were committed by government forces of the Serbian special police (MUP) or the Yugoslav Army (VJ). Under the command of Yugoslav President Slobodan Milošević, government troops have committed extrajudicial executions and other unlawful killings, systematically destroyed civilian property, and attacked humanitarian aid workers, all of which are violations of the rules of war.

The Albanian insurgency, known as the Ushtria Çlirimtare e Kosovës (UÇK, or Kosovo Liberation Army (KLA)), has also violated the laws of war by such actions as the taking of civilian hostages and by summary executions. Although on a lesser scale than the government abuses, these too are violations of international standards, and should be condemned.

The primary responsibility for gross government abuses lies with Slobodan Milošević, who rode to power in the late eighties by inciting Serbian nationalist chauvinism around the Kosovo issue. Now, after wars in Bosnia and Croatia, he has returned to the place where his post-communist career began.

Despite constant promises not to "repeat Bosnia," the international community has failed to stop Milošević's abusive campaign. The evidence even suggests that the international community, opposed to an independent Kosovo and fearful of the UÇK's rapid growth, turned a blind eye to serious abuses by the government.

The first atrocities took place in late February and early March in the Drenica region of central Kosovo, a stronghold of the UÇK. Special police forces attacked three villages with artillery, helicopters, and armored vehicles, killing at least eighty-three people, twenty-four of them women and children. Although it is unclear to what extent the UÇK was offering resistance, the evidence strongly suggests that at least seventeen people were executed after they had been detained or surrendered.

The police attack in Drenica was a watershed in the Kosovo conflict; thousands of outraged Albanians who had been committed to the nonviolent politics of their political leader Ibrahim Rugova decided to join the UÇK. In the ensuing months, the UÇK, called a "liberation movement" by most ethnic Albanians and a "terrorist organization" by the Yugoslav government, took control of an estimated 40 percent of Kosovo's territory.

The first major government offensive began in mid-May, a few days after Milošević agreed to U.S. demands that he meet with Rugova. The special police together with the Yugoslav Army attacked a string of towns and villages along the border with Albania in the west, with the specific intent of depopulating the region. Until then, the UÇK had been receiving arms and fresh recruits from across the border.

Many villages from Peć in the north to Đakovica in the south were shelled while civilians were still present. Noncombatants who fled the attacks were sometimes fired on by snipers, and a still undetermined number of people were taken into detention. In three cases, helicopters marked with the Red Cross emblem reportedly fired on civilians. Landmines were placed in strategic points along the border, as well as along the southern border with Macedonia. Most villages in the region were looted and systematically destroyed, and farmers' livestock was shot, to ensure that no one could return in the short-run. Fifteen thousand people fled to Albania and an estimated 30,000 went north to Montenegro.

The UÇK's first major offensive began on July 19 when it attempted to capture the town of Orahovac. The offensive failed, as the police recaptured the town two days later. In the fighting at least forty-two people were killed. Witnesses reported summary executions and the use of human shields by the police. Foreign journalists reported on mass graves, although these reports have not been confirmed. The extent of the abuses in Orahovac may remain unknown until the government allows an international forensics team to inspect the site.

The government forces intensified their offensive throughout July, August and September, despite promises from Milošević that it had stopped. By mid-August, the government had retaken much of the territory held by the UÇK, including their stronghold Mališevo. Unable to protect the civilian population, the UÇK retreated into Drenica and some pockets in the West and South.

The government offensive was an apparent attempt to crush civilian support for the rebels. Government forces attacked civilians, systematically destroyed towns, and forced thousands of people to flee their homes. One attack killed seventeen civilians who were hiding in the woods, and another killed three humanitarian aid workers who were trying to deliver food. The police were seen looting homes, destroying already abandoned villages, burning crops, and killing farm animals. Many people were beaten by the police or arrested after they had returned to their homes.

The majority of those killed and injured have been civilians. At least 250,000 people are currently displaced, many of them women and children now living with their families or without shelter in the mountains and woods. They face dire conditions with winter approaching. Many are too afraid to return to their homes, or have no homes to which they can return.

Despite some improvements in September, the government often hindered the ability of humanitarian aid agencies to treat the internally displaced. On various occasions, the police restricted access to needy populations, confiscated supplies, harassed and even attacked humanitarian aid workers and doctors. The government justified the restricted access by arguing that some humanitarian organizations had distributed supplies, including arms, to the UÇK.

The Yugoslav government has also restricted the work of domestic and foreign journalists who seek to report the atrocities. Some ethnic Albanian journalists have been threatened, detained, or beaten by the police. Independent radio and television stations in the Albanian language are denied licenses or, in one case, closed down.

The independent Serbian-language media is not exempt from state pressure. News wires, newspapers, and radio stations that report objectively on Kosovo are labeled "traitors" and threatened with legal action. In October, three newspapers were closed down because they violated a special government decree that censored the press in response to perceived NATO threats. As this report was going to print, the Serbian government had just passed a highly restrictive Law on Information that banned foreign broadcasts of "a political-propaganda nature" and placed exceedingly high fines on violators of the law. One newspaper was fined $230,000 for violating the law because it published an open letter that was critical of the government. As was the case during the wars in Bosnia and Croatia, the state-run radio and television purposefully spread disinformation about Kosovo and promoted images of "the enemy" intended to inflame the conflict.

The international media covering Kosovo also faces a number of restrictions on its work, starting with the denial of visas to critical journalists whom the state considers "anti-Serb." One journalist was declared persona non grata. A number of foreign journalists have been beaten or fired upon by the police.

At least one hundred ethnic Albanians have "disappeared" in Kosovo since February 1998, about half of whom were last seen in the custody of the police. The precise number is impossible to determine since the Yugoslav authorities do not make public the number of people they have in detention. Some of the "disappeared" may be in prison, others may be dead. Others unaccounted for in the conflict may be in hiding, have fled Kosovo, or have joined the UÇK.

According to the government, as of October 4, 1,242 ethnic Albanians had been charged with committing "terrorist acts," although only 684 of these people were in custody. Detained individuals include human rights activists, humanitarian aid workers, political party members, doctors, and lawyers, many of whom have been physically abused. The use of torture against detainees is widespread, and five people are known to have died from abuse in prison.

The UÇK has also committed serious violations of international humanitarian law, including the taking of hostages and extrajudicial executions. An estimated 138 ethnic Serbs, and a number of ethnic Albanians and Roma, are missing in circumstances in which UÇK involvement is suspected: at least thirty-nine of them were last seen in UÇK custody. In some villages the UÇK tried to drive ethnic Serbs from their homes. In some cases, elderly Serbs stayed behind, either too old to flee or unwilling to abandon their homes. Some of these people are currently missing and feared dead.

On September 9, the police announced that they had found thirty-four bodies of people reportedly killed by the UÇK near Glodjane. By September 16, eleven bodies had been identified, among them some ethnic Albanians. Until then, the most serious allegation of UÇK abuse was the reported execution of twenty-two Serbian civilians in the village of Klečka, where the police claimed to have discovered human remains and a kiln used to cremate the bodies. The manner in which the allegations were made, however, raised serious questions and underlined the importance of an investigation by an impartial forensic investigations team to examine Klečka, as well as the other areas where summary executions have been reported.

Despite the seriousness of these abuses in Kosovo, the international community has failed to take adequate steps to stop the killing. The U.S. government, European Union, United Nations, and NATO have all issued strong warnings, but they have failed to follow through on their threats, despite mounting abuses. Punitive measures have been slow, weak, and rapidly rescinded when Milošević offered the slightest concession.

A serious threat of NATO action came only in October, after Milošević had accomplished his military objectives and terrorized the Albanian population. As this report went to press, Milošević had agreed to a cessation of hostilites, the partial withdrawal of his security forces, and to engage in discussions on Kosovo's political status. Plans were being finalized to send a 2,000-person mission of the Organization for Security and Cooperation in Europe (OSCE) to monitor Milošević's compliance. But serious questions remain about the safety of the OSCE mission members, the strength of their mandate, and the willingness and ability of the international community to respond should the FRY government fail to comply with the terms of the agreement (*See* Appendix D).

Tolerating human rights abuses and war crimes in Kosovo will be catastrphic, not only for the Albanians and Serbs in Kosovo. An ongoing conflict will have a direct and destabilizing impact on the neighboring republic of

Montenegro, and on the bordering countries of Bosnia and Albania, already fragile, as well as Macedonia, where fighting could draw in Greece, Bulgaria, and Turkey. It also ensures that Milošević will remain the head of a corrupt and authoritarian Yugoslavia that will continue to be a threat to the region's stability.

2. RECOMMENDATIONS

To the Yugoslav Government:[1]
Compliance With Humanitarian Law

•   stop the disproportionate use of force against the civilian population and the specific targeting of civilians during military operations;

•   halt all long-range artillery shelling, and other military operations that are being used to target or indiscriminately fire on civilians;

•   stop the systematic destruction of civilian property. This includes the burning and destruction of homes, the burning of crops and the killing of livestock;

•   put an end to summary executions and prosecute any person found to have executed people in detention;

•   take all necessary steps to protect civilian populations form the effects of military operations;

---

[1] Government officials responsible for federal, republican, and local responses to the insurgency in Kosovo include:

•   Slobodan Milošević, president, Federal Republic of Yugoslavia;
•   Zoran Sokolović, minister of interior, Federal Republic of Yugoslavia;
•   Vlajko Stojković, minister of interior, Republic of Serbia;
•   Vlastimir Djordjević, head of public security department, Ministry of Interior, Republic of Serbia;
•   Dragisa Ristivojević, deputy head of public security department, Ministry of Interior, Republic of Serbia;
•   Obrad Stevanović, assistant minister of the interior, Republic of Serbia;
•   Jovica Stanisić, assistant minister of the interior and head of Serbian state security, Republic of Serbia (Stanisić was replaced by General Radomir Marković on October 27, 1998.
•   Radomir Marković, assistant minister of the interior, deputy head of state security, Republic of Serbia;
•   Frenki Simatović, chief special forces of state security, Republic of Serbia;
•   David Gajić, head of security in Kosovo, Republic of Serbia;
•   Lubinko Cvetić, deputy head of security in Kosovo, Republic of Serbia;
•   Veljko Odalović, deputy head of the Kosovo District, Republic of Serbia;

- withdraw immediately from the region all Serbian special police forces and any paramilitary units that have or are suspected of having perpetrated human rights or humanitarian law violations;

- conduct an investigation and hold accountable those members of the police and security forces found responsible for violations of human rights and international humanitarian law;

- cooperate with the International Criminal Tribunal for the Former Yugoslavia (ICTY) in its efforts to investigate alleged violations of international humanitarian law on both sides in Kosovo.

Access for Human Rights and Humanitarian Organizations

- guarantee safe passage and unincumbered access for humanitarian aid delivery and distribution;

- provide unrestricted access for the United Nations Special Rapporteur on the Former Yugoslavia to investigate violations of humanitarian law by both sides in the crisis region, as well as human rights violations;

- grant independent human rights monitors immediate full and unfettered access to the crisis region in order to investigate allegations of humanitarian and human rights violations;

- readmit the Organization for Security and Cooperation in Europe's (OSCE) long-term monitoring mission to the Federal Republic of Yugoslavia.

- provide immediate access for teams of independent forensic experts to carry out investigations into allegations of mass graves and other atrocities in the region, including in Klečka, Orahovac, Glodjane and Prekaz.

- grant full and unimpeded access to journalists covering the conflict in Kosovo.

Treatment of and Access to Detainees

- fully disclose the names of those currently detained in the course of the conflict, their ages, where they were captured, where they are being detained, and other relevant details;

- allow the International Committee for the Red Cross (ICRC) unhindered and ongoing access to all detainees, including those who are currently being investigated but have not been charged with a crime;

- guarantee that detainees have regular access to their lawyers and family members, that they are able to meet with their lawyers in private, and have adequate resources and time to prepare their defense;

- conduct an investigation into the allegations of widespread torture and ill-treatment in detention, including in particular allegations of the deaths of at least five persons as a result of torture by police. Those found responsible for such abuse should be held accountable before the law.

- undertake efforts to guarantee fair trials for all those currently in detention.

Treatment of Internally Displaced Persons

Internally displaced persons have fundamental, non-derogable rights to life and freedom from torture and other ill-treatment; rights that must be respected and ensured by any authorities on whose territory they may seek refuge. Human Rights Watch therefore calls on the responsible government officials in areas in which IDPs seek refuge to:

- receive and ensure the security and well-being of Kosovar Albanians who seek refuge in their territory. All Kosovar Albanians have a right to remain within the territory of the Federal Republic of Yugoslavia if they so choose, and may not be deported to other countries against their will;

- keep all internal borders open for and provide refuge to Kosovar Albanians who are displaced by the conflict. Displaced persons from Kosovo should only return to their homes if they voluntarily decide to do so without any government coercion.

To the Ushtria Çlirimtare e Kosovës (UÇK):

Because the fighting in Kosovo is an internal armed conflict covered by international humanitarian law, both government forces and the UÇK are obliged to respect, at a minimum, the provisions of Common Article 3 of the Geneva Conventions, which require that civilians and other protected persons be treated humanely, with specific prohibitions on murder, torture, or cruel, humiliating or degrading treatment. Human Rights Watch, therefore, calls on the UÇK to:

- respect its obligations under international law. In particular, the UÇK should release all civilians in detention, refrain from attacks on members of the civilian population and from using any detainees or civilians as hostages, and treat humanely Serbian soldiers or policemen in custody;

- condemn hostage-taking and the ill-treatment of civilians or others placed hors de combat and renounce such tactics;

- impose a code of military conduct that punishes UÇK hostage-taking, using humans as shields, and other conduct prohibited by international humanitarian law; take steps to inform troops of binding rules and that violators among UÇK troops will be held accountable;

- bring to justice commanders and troops guilty of these violations in conformity with international standards of due process;

- grant humanitarian organizations full and ongoing access to the conflict zone under UÇK control and to people in UÇK detention.

To the International Community

The international community has issued strong statements but has failed to apply the pressure necessary to convince President Slobodan Milošević to stop his abusive campaign. It is critical for the United States, the European Union, and other members of the international community to exert strong and sustained pressure on the Yugoslav leadership. Specifically, Human Rights Watch urges the international community to:

- take decisive action to stop the atrocities being committed against civilians and to ensure that the conditions set out in the Contact Group statement of March 9, including among other things the withdrawal of special police units and cessation of action by the security forces targeting the civilian population, are immediately implemented by the Yugoslav government;

- support the establishment of an international human rights monitoring mission for Kosovo under the auspices of the U.N. High Commissioner for Human Rights and insist that it be given immediate and unconditional access to the region;

- insist on immediate access for international forensic experts to undertake an investigation into allegations of mass graves and other atrocities in Kosovo;

- guarantee ongoing financial and political support to ensure that the ICTY can immediately undertake such an investigation. Further, all governments conducting intelligence operations in and around Kosovo should provide the ICTY with any evidence they obtain relating to the commission of war crimes.

- use satellite intelligence methods to monitor the region and convey relevant information to the ICTY;

- ensure that military attaches who conducted ad hoc monitoring missions to Kosovo from Belgrade on a daily basis starting in the early spring convey relevant information gathered to the ICTY;

- attach humanitarian law and human rights experts to Kosovo Diplomatic Observer Mission (KDOM), so that their inspections can be tailored to the needs of the ICTY;

- ensure that all evidence and intelligence related to Slobodan Milošević's responsibility for war crimes in Bosnia and Hercegovina, Croatia, and in Kosovo is turned over to the ICTY for investigation;

- send a clear message that war crimes, crimes against humanity, and acts of genocide will not be tolerated by arresting those already indicted by the ICTY for atrocities committed during the wars in Croatia and Bosnia;

- provide all necessary financial and political support for an intensified investigation effort by the ICTY into war crimes in Kosovo. In particular, insist that the ICTY representatives be allowed to conduct investigations, including forensic investigations, in Kosovo with unimpeded access to all sites and witnesses;

- raise awareness about the mandate of the ICTY and the obligations created by international humanitarian law in both the Serbian and Albanian languages, through e.g. publicity campaigns;

- provide all necessary financial and political support for the Office of the High Commissioner for Human Rights to increase its presence on the ground;

- insist that the ICRC is granted immediate and complete access to territory and all detainees and ensure that the government of FRY does not create artificial obstacles to impede their efforts to provide medical and other assistance to the population;

- insist that the ICRC and other humanitarian agencies are provided radio licences and allowed to import their supplies without restriction;

- press parties to acknowledge international humanitarian law obligations and agree to abide by them;

- impose a moratorium on return of refugees, rejected asylum seekers and others to the territory of the Federal Republic of Yugoslavia;

- provide adequate international assistance so that refugees and displaced persons can be received in Bosnia, Albania, Montenegro and other countries to which they may flee; and

- increase financial assistance to organizations providing humanitarian relief in Kosovo.

In addition to the recommendations to the international community at large, Human Rights Watch calls on the following international actors to use the authority of their respective institutions or governments to address the serious human rights crisis in Kosovo. Specifically,

To the United Nations:

The ongoing conflict in Kosovo—with the mounting evidence of atrocities and concomitant displacement of the population—is a dangerous threat to regional stability and security. Human Rights Watch, therefore, calls on the United Nations Security Council to implement the recommendations made above to the international community at large, and to:

- ensure the implementation of its own resolutions 1160 and 1199, of March and September 1998 respectively, which called for, among other things, an immediate cessation of hostilities and for the president of FRY to implement his own commitments from the June 16 joint statement with the president of the Russian Federation not to carry out any repressive actions against the peaceful population, to facilitate refugee return, and to cooperate with the ICTY;

- on the occasion of the next secretary-general's report on the situation in Kosovo, hold an open debate within the Security Council to discuss the contents of that report and the necessary steps to remedy the abuses documented therein;

- call on the government of Slobodan Milošević to invite the U.N. Special Rapporteur on Extrajudicial, Summary or Arbitrary Executions and the U.N. Working Group on Arbitrary Detention and the Working Group on Disappearances urgently to conduct an investigation in Kosovo and report back to the Security Council;

- facilitate and encourage the work of the ICTYugoslavia to investigate alleged violations of international humanitarian law in Kosovo and guarantee ongoing financial and political support to ensure that the Tribunal can immediately undertake such an investigation;

- compel the FRY government to cooperate with the ICTY by adopting measures necessary under Yugoslav law to implement the provisions of Security Council Resolution 827 and the statutes of the Tribunal, transferring to the Tribunal custody those indicted persons on Yugoslav territory, and facilitate an independent investigation in to allegations of war crimes in the recent conflict in Kosovo.

To the General Assembly:
>Human Rights Watch calls on the General Assembly of the United Nations, which will be considering the report by the Special Rapporteur on the Former Yugoslavia later this fall, to:

- condemn the ongoing commission of atrocities and address any of the outstanding human rights and humanitarian issues in Kosovo;

- call on the Yugoslav government to accept, and the U.N. to fund, the establishment of a monitoring office based in Priština under the auspices of the U.N. High Commissioner for Human Rights.

To the High Commissioner for Human Rights:
>Human Rights Watch urges the U.N. High Commissioner for Human Rights Mary Robinson to:

- seek to establish an office in Kosovo to monitor abuses of human rights and international humanitarian law;

- use her authority to encourage U.N. treaty bodies and mechanisms to be engaged in Kosovo and to facilitate their access to the region.

To the International Criminal Tribunal for the former Yugoslavia:
- dispatch a high-level delegation, including Chief Justice Arbour, to Belgrade and Priština to put both sides on notice of the Tribunal's jurisdiction and the likely repercussions of international humanitarian law violations;

- intensify efforts to investigate atrocities being committed in Kosovo, including by dispatching teams of investigators to Kosovo, as well as to refugee-receiving areas such as Montenegro, Macedonia, and Albania to interview victims and eye witnesses to atrocities;

- ensure that witnesses, particularly those still based in Kosovo, are provided with adequate protection;

To the United State Government:
- work with allies to enforce sanctions that target the ruling elite and hold firm on conditions set for lifting of any sanctions;

- continue and enhance support for the ICTY;

- ensure that efforts to provide humanitarian assistance entail adequate security measures for displaced persons;

To the European Union:
- agree to a moratorium on the return of refugees, rejected asylum seekers and displaced persons to the Federal Republic of Yugoslavia;

- provide assistance to enable adequate protection in region so that refugees and displaced persons can be received in Bosnia, Montenegro, Albania and other countries to which they may flee;

- take steps to improve sanctions that target the ruling elite, including prompt and unwavering imposition of all future sanctions endorsed by the Contact Group, the Security Council and other multilateral fora;

To the Russian Federation:
- cease obstruction of international efforts to sanction and condemn the violence in Kosovo;

- use its special relationship with the Federal Republic of Yugoslavia to communicate to authorities that international humanitarian law and human rights violations in Kosovo cannot be tolerated and to obtain agreement by the FRY government on measures outlined above.

To the Organization for Security and Cooperation in Europe:
- insist that Kosovo is a primary focus of the Special Representative of the OSCE to the Federal Republic of Yugoslavia, Felipe Gonzalez;

- ensure that OSCE monitors stationed in northern Albania and Macedonia convey to the Tribunal relevant information, including, for example, any evidence they have of the use of air power on fleeing civilians;

To the Council of Europe:
- send a clear message to the government of the Federal Republic of Yugoslavia that there will be no consideration of its application for accession to the Council of Europe until it stops committing atrocities in

Kosovo and makes a sincere commitment to abide by the Council's human rights standards throughout its territory.

3. VIOLATIONS IN THE DRENICA REGION

Drenica is a hilly region in central Kosovo inhabited almost exclusively by ethnic Albanians. The region has a tradition of strong resistance to outside powers, dating back to Turkish rule in the Balkans. By late 1997, Albanians had begun to refer to Drenica as "liberated territory" because of the local UÇK presence, which forced Serbian policemen to abandon their checkpoints at night. The government considered Drenica the hotbed of "Albanian terrorism."

A focal point of police attention in Drenica was the village of Donji Prekaz, and especially the family compound of Adem Jashari, who was gaining repute in 1997 as a local UÇK leader. In January and then again in March 1998, the police mounted attacks on the compound, the second involving a large-scale force based at the nearby ammunition factory. Jashari's entire family, save an eleven-year-old girl, was killed in the attack. Of fifty-eight bodies later buried, eighteen were women and ten were children sixteen years old or younger.

On February 28 and March 1, the police mounted a major attack on two other villages in Drenica: Ćirez and Likošane. In both cases, special police forces attacked without warning, firing indiscriminately at women, children and other noncombatants. Helicopters and military vehicles sprayed village rooftops with gunfire before police forces entered the village on foot, firing into private homes. A pregnant woman, Rukia Nebihi, was shot in the face, and four brothers from one family were killed, apparently while in police custody. Ten members of the Ahmeti family were summarily executed by the police (see below).

The Serbian police denied any wrongdoing in the attacks and claimed they were pursuing "terrorists" who had attacked the police. A police spokesman denied the "lies and inventions" about torture carried by some local and foreign media and said "the police has never resorted to such methods and never will."[2]

These events in Drenica, in which eighty-three people died, including at least twenty-four women and children, were the turning point in the Kosovo crisis. Although the size and structure of the UÇK was unknown up to that point, there is no question that the brutal and indiscriminate attacks on women and children greatly radicalized the ethnic Albanian population and swelled the ranks of the armed insurgency. Whether Milošević thought he could crush the UÇK in Drenica, or whether he intended for the UÇK to grow and become more aggressive is a question for debate.

---

[2]"Interior Ministry Spokesman Gives Press Conference," Tanjug, March 7, 1998.

The Attack on Likošane

The first large-scale police attacks in Drenica were on Likošane and Ćirez, small villages that lie about two kilometers apart from one another, on February 28 and March 1. From the testimonies of victims, witnesses, and those who visited the villages just after the attack, it is clear that the special police forces used at least one attack helicopter, armored personnel carriers (APCs), mortars, and automatic machine guns in the attack.

Twenty-five ethnic Albanians died in the attack. Although it is unknown how much resistance was mounted by the local villagers and the UÇK, most of the Albanians who died were clearly not offering any resistance at the time of their death. Evidence strongly suggests that the police summarily executed at least fourteen people.

It is still not clear how and why the attack began. According to a police spokesman, a police patrol was attacked by armed Albanians near Likošane on February 28; four policemen were killed and two seriously injured. A fight ensued over the next two days, in which sixteen "terrorists" and two policemen were killed.[3] A report by the pro-government Media Center in Priština said that there were three simultaneous attacks on the police near Likošane on February 28. Police officers Miroslav Vujković and Goran Radojčić were killed, while officers Pavle Damjanović and Slaviša Matejić were wounded and later died. Sixteen Albanians were also killed.[4]

Albanians from Likošane and Ćirez told Human Rights Watch that they heard shooting near Likošane, at the place called "Six Oaks," around 11:00 a.m. on February 28, and some had heard that the police had been ambushed there. There were also unconfirmed reports that armed Albanians had attacked the ammunition plant near Donji Prekaz, where the police were based, on February 27. When the police chased the Albanians, they were ambushed near Likošane.

Regardless of what triggered the incident, there is no question that the special police forces acted in a quick and well-organized manner, which suggests that the police may have been planning to attack. There is also no doubt that the police used arbitrary and excessive force against the villagers long after resistance had ceased.

Some articles in the Western press cited anonymous Serbian police sources who said that, while the Albanians had fired first, the situation had then

---

[3]"Interior Ministry Spokesman Gives Press Conference," Tanjug March 7, 1998.

[4]"Dialogue not Separatism and Terrorism," Media Center, Priština, Yugoslavia, May 1998.

gotten "out of hand."[5] One article cited an unnamed Serbian police officer as saying that only intervention by a Belgrade commander had limited the slaughter of villagers.[6]

According to those present in Likošane, the police arrived in the village between 11:30 a.m. and 12:00 p.m., about half an hour after the shots had been heard near Six Oaks. An attack helicopter was firing overhead while APCs and many armed special police surrounded the village. Villagers told Human Rights Watch that there was no UÇK presence, but it is possible that someone was firing at the police.

Two neighboring households were the focus of police attacks: the families Gjeli and Ahmeti. Two men were killed by gunshots in the former, eleven in the latter, apparently while in police custody.

At around 3:30 p.m. the police burst into the compound of the Ahmeti family, which was the richest family in Likošane. There is some speculation that an UÇK member may have entered the house and then left, but it remains unclear why the Ahmeti house was targeted. Interviews conducted by Human Rights Watch, the Humanitarian Law Center, the Council for the Defense of Human Rights and Freedoms, an ethnic Albanian human rights group, and foreign journalists corroborate a story of beatings and, ultimately, the extrajudicial executions of ten Ahmeti men, aged between sixteen and fifty, as well as one family guest, Bajram Fazliu.

According to two women in the Ahmeti family interviewed by the Humanitarian Law Center, the police, dressed in green and blue camouflage uniforms, broke down the family compound gate with an armored vehicle and then broke into the house. The police ordered everyone to lie down on the floor, and then the men were taken outside the compound, where they were beaten. Two neighbors of the Ahmeti family, Ilir Islami and Haxhi Hasani, told the Council for the Defense of Human Rights and Freedoms that they heard the screams of the Ahmeti men from the front yard until the evening.

One woman in the house, Merci Ahmeti, told a journalist from the *Times*:

> All of our men walked out to protect the rest of us. The police
> beat them unconscious. Then they told us to lie on the ground
> and kept some policemen to watch over us for the next four

---

[5]Reuters, March 2, 1998.

[6]Guy Dinmore, "Serbian Forces Accused of Slaughter," *Financial Times*, March 3, 1998.

hours. We heard screams outside and shots. We do not know
what happened, but I knew then they were no longer alive.[7]

The only brother to survive the attack, Xhevdet Ahmeti, was by chance
in Priština on February 28. The next day, having learned of the incident, he
returned to Likošane and watched from a hill overlooking the village as the police
continued their attack. He told Human Rights Watch:

I arrived around 8 a.m. on March 1. There was an APC in our
compound and another outside. A third was behind. There was
artillery all over and the police were shooting everywhere.[8]

According to Xhevdet Ahmeti, the police withdrew around 3:30 p.m. He
immediately went to his house and was told that the police had taken ten male
members of his family and Bajram Fazliu into custody. He told Human Rights
Watch that the doors and furniture of the house had been destroyed, and that the
police had taken most of the family's valuables, such as the television satellite dish,
clothing, and shoes that their uncle had just brought back from Switzerland, as well
as some gold and 50,000 Swiss francs.

Xhevdet and the rest of the Ahmeti family did not learn that the eleven
men in custody had been killed until March 2, when their bodies were seen by
chance in the Priština morgue by another Likošane resident, Kadri Gjeli, who had
gone to collect two members of his family who had been killed (see below). An
Ahmeti cousin then went to the morgue himself to collect the bodies. On his
return, he was blocked by the police in Komoran and was forced to take a
circuitous route by unpaved roads.

The eleven men were buried on March 3, along with the fifteen other
victims from Likošane and Ćirez. A journalist from the United States who saw the
Ahmeti corpses on May 2 told Human Rights Watch that they bore clear signs of
torture, including gouged out eyes and slash wounds.[9] Autopsies were not

---

[7]Tom Walker, "Massacre by the 'Ethnic Cleansers'," *Times* (London), March 4,
1998.

[8]Human Rights Watch interview with Xhevdet Ahmeti, Likošane, May 24, 1998.

[9]Human Rights Watch telephone interview with Chris Hedges, June 16, 1998. See
Chris Hedges, "Albanians Bury 24 Villagers Slain by the Serbs," *New York Times*, March
3, 1998.

performed on any of the victims, even though Article 252 of the Yugoslav Criminal Code mandates autopsies in cases where the death may have been related to a criminal act. On April 3, lawyers for the Ahmeti family asked the local prosecutor and investigating judge to investigate why the autopsies had never been performed but, as of September 1998, they had received no answer. As of September 1998, the Ahmeti family had still not received death certificates from the local authorities despite repeated requests by their lawyers.

It is not clear whether the Ahmeti men and Bajram Fazliu were killed in Likošane in front of the Ahmeti family compound or after they had been taken away by the police. A researcher for the Humanitarian Law Center, who was in Likošane on March 2, saw blood, teeth, and what looked like brain tissue near the bushes in front of the front gates, which suggests some or all of the men were either killed or severely beaten in front of the compound. Human Rights Watch spoke separately with two journalists, an ethnic Albanian and an American, who both saw the same blood and human remains in front of the Ahmeti's gates on March 2, as well as Serbian writing on the compound wall that said: "This is what will happen next time too."[10]

The other household in Likošane targeted by the police was that of seventy-year-old Muhamet Gjeli, who, according to the Albanian-language media, had been deported from Germany on December 17, 1998.[11] Muhamet and his son Naser were apparently killed by gunshots, Muhamet in a small dairy next to his house and Naser inside the house in front of his wife and two children, aged two and four. It is not known whether the two men were shooting at the police or whether the police warned them to surrender before shooting.

Naser's wife, Ganimete Islami, told the Council for the Defense of Human Rights and Freedoms that she first heard shooting from Six Oaks around 12:00 p.m., so she took her children into the bathroom while her husband joined them with a hunting rifle and put a mattress over the window. She said:

> At one moment, bullets got through the windows and shot my husband dead. Bullets came through the door, too. The firing stopped and the room was full of steam and dust...

---

[10]Humanitarian Law Center, Spotlight Report No. 26, "Kosovo: Human Rights in Times of Armed Conflict," May 1998. See also Philip Smucker, "Evidence Grows that Serb Police Units Carried Out Summary Executions," *The Daily Telegraph*, March 4, 1998.

[11]"Viktima e Likoshanit ishte debuar nga Gjermania gjate dhjetori te vjetme," *Koha Ditore*, May 1998.

Muhamet was apparently killed in the small dairy next to the house. Journalists who visited the scene saw an axe, a cap, and a blood smear indicating that the body had been dragged out of the dairy.[12] According to Ganimete Islami, the police took Naser and Muhamet's bodies, as well as 6,500 DM from the house. They also destroyed the family's tractor and Zastava car.

The Attack on Ćirez

According to those present on February 28, the police arrived in Ćirez around 12:30 p.m., after the shooting near Six Oaks. Three witnesses independently told Human Rights Watch that at least seven APCs were present, as well as a helicopter which was firing down on rooftops.[13] Damage of the buildings in Ćirez seen by Human Rights Watch was consistent with those claims.

The most brutal incident was the killing of Rukia Nebihu, a twenty-seven-year-old woman who was seven months pregnant. Her father-in-law, Sefer Nebihu, was present with his wife, eldest son, Xhemsil, and five children when the police shot Rukia in the face, killing her instantly. Xhemsil was also killed. Sefer Nebihu told Human Rights Watch:

> The police destroyed my front gate with two tanks and came up to the windows of my house. About seventeen policemen came out of the tanks. They wore military camouflage, green and yellow, with a police sign on their chests. No masks. The tank came up to the window. One policeman broke the window with the butt of his gun and started shouting. They said "stand up" and I said "don't shoot because there are only women and children here." They cursed me and then one fired at me.[14]

Sefer Nebihu was hit three times in the right leg and one time in the left. Human Rights Watch saw the bullet scars, which were consistent with an automatic gun having been sprayed at about thigh level. All of the bullet marks were between

---

[12]See, for example, Guy Dinmore, "Serbian Forces Accused of Slaughter," *Financial Times*, March 3, 1998.

[13]In a press conference on March 7, Ministry of Internal Affairs spokesman Colonel Ljubinko Cvetić told journalists that helicopters were only used for humanitarian purposes, such as for evacuating the injured.

[14]Human Rights Watch interview with Sefer Nebihu, Ćirez, May 24, 1998.

the knees and groin. According to Sefer, he fell back and Rukia grabbed his leg while he was on the ground. He said:

> Rukia grabbed my leg and saw what happened as they smashed the side door. When the door was smashed, Rukia was holding my leg. They shot her and hit her in the face... After they shot Rukia, they said "What is he doing here?" and they fired at Xhemsil. I think there were fifteen to seventeen bullet holes in his stomach. He [the policeman] kept shooting until the magazine was empty. Then they [the police] entered all of the rooms checking everything. Seventeen policemen were inside, one was outside with a Motorola [radio]. I heard him say "where now?"

After the shooting, the police took Sefer to the house next door where his other son, twenty-one-year-old Zahir, was hiding. Sefer was told to call his son, which he did. He said:

> One [policeman] tried to hit him [Zahir] with the butt of his gun in the head but he ducked and it hit him in the chest. They told him to lie down. They forced me to open all the rooms in the house and they searched everything.
>
> They took me to my brother's house and they asked who lives there. Inside the house were twenty-three women and children. I told them to come out. They came out and were told to lay down on the grass. One policeman came running up and said "kill them all." They started arguing amongst themselves and some of them said "we can't shoot them."

Sefer's other son, Ilir, who was the husband of Rukia, was also taken by the police from somewhere in the village during the attack in Ćirez. His corpse was returned to Ćirez on March 2 along with the other twenty-five victims from Likošane and Ćirez. It is not known when or how he died.

Four other victims from Ćirez were the sons of the Sejdiu family, Bekim, Nazmi, Bedri, and Beqir, who were apparently executed by the police outside of their home. According to Abida Sejdiu, the mother of the household, her sons came back from working in the fields when they heard the shooting near Likošane around 12:00 p.m.. Around 3:30 p.m. some APCs slammed open the family's front gates. Visibly disturbed, she told Human Rights Watch:

> They [her sons] came from the field and we sat in one room. My daughter-in-law, two kids and my sons. They [the police] surrounded the house. We heard fighting in Likošane around noon. My sons were killed around 4 p.m. The tanks came in the garden, they broke the gates and two tanks were outside the compound and two behind. Two helicopters were constantly firing. Some seven to ten policemen broke into the house and our room. I stepped in front of the police and put my hands out in front of my sons. They took all of us into the garden. They said lie on the ground. They hit Bekim and I shouted "Don't you have any sons!" They hit me on the head with the end of the gun. They took all of my sons then I took the kids inside...[15]

At this point, Mrs. Sejdiu could say no more and left the room. Her husband, Sheremet said that she had witnessed her sons being killed. According to him, the police killed Nazmi first. Then they took Bekim outside and shot him in the garden, followed by Bedri and Beqir. He told Human Rights Watch that Beqir had seventeen bullets in his chest. The police didn't take the bodies. Human Rights Watch saw photographs of two of the Sejdiu brothers, each with bullet wounds, although it was not possible to determine from this the circumstances of their deaths.

Also killed in Ćirez on March 1 in unknown circumstances were Ibish Rama, Smail Bajrami, Rexhep Rexhepi, Beqir Rexhepi, and Shaban Muja. Ibish Rama and Smail Bajrami were last seen in police custody.

According to Liman Ademi, a local villager, he, Ibish Rama, and Smail Bajrami, were hiding along with three others in a warehouse in the center of Ćirez when the police attack began around 12:30 p.m.. After one hour with machine gun fire and a helicopter shooting over head, the three of them decided to leave the warehouse and hide in the village. Liman Ademi told Human Rights Watch what happened next:

> Three of us went in one direction. Me and Ibish went towards our homes. Smail came with us because his sister lives in the same village. But the three of us found ourselves in front of an

---

[15]Human Rights Watch interview with Abida Sejdiu, Ćirez, May 24, 1998.

APC. They [the police] said lie down and one policeman got out
of the APC. We were handcuffed together and guns were
pointed at us. They took us inside the APC and we drove to the
main road. One policeman went out of the APC and called
some other policeman. I was closest to the door. They untied
me and I went outside with one policeman and he told me to
wait there, but the other one was aiming his gun at me. Then the
APC started to move slowly [because there was a disturbance
somewhere else]. The other cop started to move away from me
slowly. At that moment, the other cop aiming at me turned
away. I took the chance and ran away. My two friends were
still tied inside the APC. Three days later I found out that my
two friends were massacred along with twelve others.[16]

On March 3, all twenty-six people killed in Likošane and Ćirez were
buried in a field near the two villages. An estimated 30,000 people attended the
ceremony. Police checkpoints on the major road from Komoran prohibited many
more from coming. Visitors from outside the area and journalists had to
circumvent the police by back roads and walking through fields.

The Attacks on Donji Prekaz
Human Rights Watch was not able to visit Donji Prekaz, a village with a
pre-war population of approximately 1,000 people, due to continued fighting. It
is, therefore, the case from Drenica on which the least direct testimony was
available to Human Rights Watch. This notwithstanding, Human Rights Watch has
concluded that serious violations of international humanitarian law were committed
by the Serbian special police: notably, indiscriminate attacks on noncombatants, the
systematic destruction of civilian property, and the summary and arbitrary
executions of those in detention.[17] Although it appears that some Albanian
villagers in Donji Prekaz were armed and defending themselves against the police,

---

[16]Human Rights Watch interview with Liman Ademi, Ćirez, May 24, 1998.

[17]This conclusion is founded on Human Rights Watch interviews with journalists
and human rights researchers, reports by other human rights organizations, notably Amnesty
International and the Humanitarian Law Center, as well as newspaper reports and the
analysis of photographs. See Amnesty International, "A Human Rights Crisis in Kosovo
Province, Document Series A: Violence in Drenica, February-April 1998," London, June
1998, and Humanitarian Law Center, Spotlight Report No. 26.

the evidence is overwhelming that the police used excessive and indiscriminate force, and that the police executed at least three people after they had been detained or had surrendered.

The first attack on Donji Prekaz took place on January 22, 1998, and was focused on the compound of Shaban Jashari, whose son Adem was known as a local UÇK leader. Adem Jashari had already been convicted in absentia by a Priština court on July 11, 1997, for "terrorist acts" along with fourteen other ethnic Albanians, in a trial that clearly failed to conform to international standards.[18]

According to the Serbian Ministry of Internal Affairs, the January 22 incident was a shoot-out between local gangs. However, according to Shaban Jashari, who was interviewed a few days after the first incident by the Humanitarian Law Center and was killed in the second police attack, the police attacked his home around 5:30 a.m. but were repelled when Adem's friends "from the woods" came to help.[19]

Others were also victims of what appears to have been execution-style killings after detention or in unknown circumstances. Hysen Manxholli, a fifty-two-year-old ethnic Albanian from the nearby town of Srbica was killed on January 22 in unknown circumstances. His body was found the same day near the ammunition factory. According to the Council for the Defense of Human Rights and Freedoms and the Humanitarian Law Center, Idriz Idrizi was seized by the police on January 23 near the ammunition factory and, as of September 1998, was still missing.[20]

The police attacked Prekaz and the Jashari compound again on March 5, 1998, this time in a more prepared and determined manner. All evidence suggests that the attack was not intended to apprehend armed Albanians, considered "terrorists" by the government, but, as Amnesty International concluded in its report on violence in Drenica, "to eliminate the suspects and their families."[21]

---

[18]See press release, "Human Rights Watch/Helsinki Condemns Political Trial in Kosovo," July 15, 1997. The three defendants that were present for the trial, Besim Rama, Idriz Asllani, and Avni Nura, all stated that they had "confessed" after being tortured. All of the defendants were sentenced to prison terms ranging between four and twenty years.

[19]Humanitarian Law Center, Spotlight Report No. 26, Kosovo.

[20]"Enforced Disappearances in Kosovo January-May 1998," Humanitarian Law Center.

[21]Amnesty International, "A Human Rights Crisis in Kosovo Province, Document Series A: Violence in Drenica, February-April 1998," London, June 1998.

Testimonies collected by human rights groups and journalists indicate several cases of extrajudicial executions and unlawful killings from excessive force.

An estimated fifty-eight ethnic Albanians were killed in the attack, including eighteen women and ten children under the age of sixteen, and then summarily buried by the police before autopsies could be performed. The exact number and identities of the dead reported by different sources varies slightly, a consequence of the manner in which the burial was conducted (see below) and because some of the bodies were burned beyond recognition.[22] Among those buried were at least six Albanians who were killed in unclear circumstances in the nearby village of Lauša and buried together with the dead from Donji Prekaz.

According to the Serbian police, the attack on Donji Prekaz was in response to UÇK attacks on nearby police patrols. According to witnesses, however, the attack was well orchestrated and included APCs, artillery shelling from the nearby ammunition factory, and special police forces in camouflage and face paint. The first target was the Ljushtaku family compound, which is between the Jashari compound and the ammunition factory. The Ljushtaku family members fled their home as the police turned the focus of their attack on the compound of Shaban Jashari.

Based on interviews with witnesses, the Humanitarian Law Center confirmed that inside the house were, at least, Shaban Jashari (74), his wife Zaha (72), and their sons Rifat, Hamza (47), and Adem (42) with their families, including four girls, Blerina (7), Fatime (8), Besarte (11) and Lirije (14), and four boys, Blerim (12), Besim (16), Afete (17), and Selvete (20). All of these people died except Besarte, who hid under a marble slab used for kneading dough during the attack. Besarte was later captured by the police, taken to the nearby ammunition factory and then released. Interviewed later by a foreign journalist, Besarte told of hours-long shelling which killed her seven brothers and sisters, her mother and uncle Adem inside the house. "I tried to pretend I was dead," she told

---

[22]According to Amnesty International, fifty-six bodies were buried on March 11, forty-one of which were identified. Of these, twelve were women, eleven were children under sixteen, and at least two people came from Lauša. According to the Humanitarian Law Center, at least fifty-five people were buried, thirty-seven identified and eighteen unidentified. Among these were seven women, eleven children and five people from Lauša. The Albanian-language daily Koha Ditore wrote on March 9 that, in Donji Prekaz alone, forty-six people died, including eleven children, eleven women and five elderly (above seventy years old). The account of the local Council for the Defense of Human Rights and Freedoms is the most detailed, and is cited further below.

a journalist from the *Sunday Times*. "But one of the soldiers put his hand on my chest and he felt I was alive."[23]

Also killed in the attack, and probably in Shaban Jashari's house, were Adem Jashari's wife Adilje, their son Kushtrim (13), Rifat Jashari's wife, Zafire Batir, and their daughter Igballe (11), and Hamza Jashari's wife Feride Ramadan and their child Fatusha (8).

The police also attacked the homes of other Jashari family members in the village, including those of Sherif, Zuk, Qazim, Fejzija, and Beqir Jashari (43). The daughter of Serif Jashari, who was hiding in the house of Beqir Jashari together with twenty-four children, five women, and six men, told the Humanitarian Law Center that the police surrounded the house with APCs, shelled the roof and then fired tear gas into the house. She told the center:

> The soldiers shouted for us to come out one by one or they would kill us. When my cousin Qazim (47) came out with his hands up, they killed him on the steps. I was in the middle of the yard when it happened. We ran and had just gone through the first cordon when the soldiers caught my cousin Nazim (27) who was helping his mother Bahtije along. They grabbed him, tore off the woman's dress we had given him to wear, ordered him to lie down on the ground and then to get up. He had to do this many times. They fired into the back of his head and back and I saw his body jerking from the bullets.[24]

Bahtije Jashari, who also witnessed the killing of Qazim Jashari, told center staff about her son's death:

> My son Nazim took a child of one and a half years to hide him from the police and tried to help me along because I didn't have my crutch. The police grabbed him by both arms and stopped him from helping me. I begged them to let him go. They ordered my son to lie down and then searched him for guns. Then they ordered him to stand up with his hands in the air. It lasted only a few seconds. I clutched my head and started

---

[23]Marie Colvin, "Kosovo's Silent Houses of the Dead," *Sunday Times*, March 15, 1998.

[24]Humanitarian Law Center, Spotlight Report No. 26, Kosovo.

screaming. All of a sudden, the police ordered Nazim to lie down again and emptied a whole magazine into his back. They didn't let me turn him face up. A policeman told me to get away from there but I didn't. I looked at my son for the last time and said good-bye to him.[25]

The Humanitarian Law Center interviewed three people who witnessed Qazim and Nazim's executions. A forensic pathologist who examined a photograph of Nazim Jashari's body for Amnesty International found injuries "broadly consistent with the accounts of him having been extrajudicially executed."[26]

Amnesty International also interviewed most of the family groups that hid in Beqir Jashari's house and found their testimonies largely corroborated details of the attack and the extrajudicial execution of three of the six men who were with them, as well as the wounding of a fourth.

Forced Burial

On March 8, 1998, the police contacted the local Council for the Defense of Human Rights and Freedoms in Srbica and told them to take the bodies of those killed in Donji Prekaz. The council asked for the list of people killed and the appropriate documentation but were provided nothing. According to the Council, the police had transferred forty-six of the corpses to the Priština hospital morgue on March 7, and then brought them back to Srbica the next day, where they were eventually placed in a warehouse without walls on the outskirts of town.[27] Among the fifty-eight bodies were those of eight children aged seven to sixteen, and thirteen women, as well as a number of elderly. Ten corpses remained unidentifiable.[28]

Photographs taken at this time of the corpses reveal serious disfigurement and deep burns, probably from explosions. Shaban Jashari had a large hole in his

---

[25]Ibid.

[26]Amnesty International, "A Human Rights Crisis in Kosovo Province, Document Series A: Violence in Drenica, February-April 1998."

[27]Council for Defense of Human Rights and Freedoms, "Appeal on the Latest Events in Skenderaj," Priština, March 9, 1998.

[28]Council for Defense of Human Rights and Freedoms, "Quarterly Report January-March, 1998," Priština, April 17, 1998.

chest with burn marks and was missing his right hand. There were a number of dead children, including a baby, some of them burned almost beyond recognition. Adem Jashari had a bullet wound in his neck.

On March 9, the police warned publicly that they would bury the victims themselves if they were not buried by family members quickly. Family members waited in the hope that autopsies would be conducted so, on March 10, the police dug a large grave with a bulldozer near Donji Prekaz and buried fifty-six people, ten of them still unidentified.

That same day, relatives of the deceased, a group of Albanian doctors from Priština, religious leaders from the Islamic community and the Catholic church, and international aid agencies like the ICRC were denied access to Drenica by the police. ICRC also tried to act as an intermediary between the police and the families but was turned down by the authorities.[29] Police spokesman Ljubinko Cvetić, in a press conference in Priština, told reporters that humanitarian aid agencies had been turned back because they had been caught with weapons in the past. The head of the Secretary of Information in Kosovo, Boško Drobnjak, later told Human Rights Watch the same story.[30]

The next day, March 11, the bodies were disinterred by relatives and reburied in accordance with Islamic tradition, with the heads pointed towards Mecca. None of the bodies showed signs that autopsies had been performed, even though Yugoslav law stipulates that autopsies should be conducted when there is reason to believe that the death was connected to a criminal act.[31]

On March 13, the United States-based human rights group Physicians for Human Rights (PHR), which conducted autopsies in Bosnia, requested twelve visas from the Yugoslav authorities for an international team of forensics experts it had assembled to investigate the deaths in Donji Prekaz, Likošane and Ćirez. In addition, the prosecutor for the ICTY requested visas for PHR and asked that its staff accompany the team to Kosovo.[32] In mid-April, the Yugoslav government responded to PHR, via the U.S. State Department, that three U.S. citizens could

---

[29]Associated Press, March 10, 1998.

[30]Human Rights Watch interview with Boško Drobnjak, Priština, June 11, 1998.

[31]Yugoslav Code of Criminal Procedure, Article 252.

[32]According to the Dayton Accords, signed by the Federal Republic of Yugoslavia, the Yugoslav government is obliged to cooperate fully with ICTY and to comply with requests for investigations into alleged war crimes.

travel to the region as long as they were accompanied by "experts" designated by the Yugoslav government, an offer that PHR did not accept.[33]

The Council for the Defense of Human Rights and Freedoms later compiled a list of those who were identified as having died in Donji Prekaz from March 5-7, as well as some Albanians killed in unclear circumstances in the nearby village of Lausha. They are:

From Donji Prekaz
Shaban Murat Jashari (74)
Zahide Jashari (72)
Hamëz Shaban Jashari (47)
Adem Shaban Jashari (42)
Zarife Bahtir Jashari (49)
Feride Jashari (43)
Adile Bahtir Jashari (40)
Hidajete Rifat Jashari (18)
Igballe Rifat Jashari (13)
Igballe Rifat Jashari (11)
Valdete Rifat Jashari (14)
Selvete Hamëz Jashari (20)
Besim Hamëz Jashari (16)
Afete Hamëz Jashari (17)
Blerim Hamëz Jashari (12)
Fatime Hamëz Jashari (8)
Blerina Hamëz Jashari (7)
Lirije Hamëz Jashari (14)
Fitim Adem Jashari (17)
Kushtrim Adem Jashari (13)
Elheme Jashari (57)
Blerim Zenë Jashari (16)
Bujar Zenë Jashari (12)
Abdullah Zenë Jashari
Hajzer Zymer Jashari (20)
Halit Imer Jashari (65)
Qazim Osman Jashari (47)
Nazmi Zukë Jashari (26)
Sinan Ramadan Jashari (66)

Ali Ramadan Jashari (68)
Feride Ramadan Jashari (43)
Beqir Bajram Jashari (43)
Halil Bajram Jashari (35)
Sherif Brahim Jashari (47)
Bahtije Muharrem Jashari (45)
Murtez Zymber Jashari (22)
Faik Tahir Jashari (30)
Qerim Husë Jashari (54)
Salë Hajzer Jashari (60)
Kajtaz Jashari (44)
Hamit H. Jashari (65)
Isak Halili (35)

From Lauša
Osman Shaban Geci (?)
Sadik Miran Kaçkini (38)
Miftar Rreci (43)
Fatime Gashi (46)
Gazmend Bajram Gashi (16)
Makfirete Bajram Gashi (13)

[33]Physicians for Human Rights press release, April 28, 1998.

The Attack on Novi Poklek

On May 31, an estimated 300 special police forces attacked Novi Poklek, a relatively wealthy village next to the small city of Glogovac. Ten men were seized by the police during the attack; one of them was found dead later that day and the other nine are still missing and are presumed dead. An eyewitness claims he saw five of these men being shot by the police, although this could not be confirmed.

How the attack began remains unclear. According to ethnic Albanians from Novi Poklek who spoke with Human Rights Watch, a car with two policemen had an accident near the village. Two villagers, Ajet Gashi and Shefqit Bytyci, went to give the plainclothes policemen some help. One of them reportedly heard the policeman in the car radio for help, saying that they had come under attack. While Human Rights Watch was not able to confirm this story, and it thus remains unclear why the police attacked Novi Poklek, there is no question of the abuses that followed.

According to three separate eyewitnesses, the police attack lasted from 12:15 p.m. to 8:00 p.m. and involved an estimated twenty-two vehicles, both APCs and jeeps, from a base at the nearby ferrous-nickel plant. The witnesses told Human Rights Watch that the police went from house to house and gathered the men and women of the village. About sixty women and children and ten men were then forced into the house of Sahit Qorri. The women and children were later released and told to run for the neighboring village of Vasiljevo. One of the ten men, seventeen-year-old Ardian Deliu, was found dead that evening after the police had left, while the other nine men are still missing.

One man from Novi Poklek claimed to have witnessed most of the attack from behind a stone wall about 200 meters from the center of the village. He testified that he saw the police shoot five people from behind, but Human Rights Watch was not able to corroborate the story. He said:

> The village was surrounded by about three hundred policemen with artillery. I saw it with my own eyes, about twenty-two vehicles were in the village. Four to five policemen entered each house and I saw the police forcing people out of their homes. They gathered them together in front of one house [Sahit Qorri's] at the entrance of the village and made them go into the house. Ten men and I don't know how many women and children, probably between sixty or seventy.

They burned one house in the center of the village. I don't know whose house because I only saw the flames. After one hour they led the women and children out of the village and forced them to Vasiljevo. Then they burned two or three more houses. And then the shooting began from all directions. It was about 4:00 or 4:30 p.m..

Then two men, Ahmet Berisha and Hajriz Hajdini, were taken out of the house. They told them to walk in the other direction from the women and children. While they were walking, it was sixty or seventy meters away, they started shooting. I just saw them falling, and I could see their backs, and they didn't get up. Ten minutes later another neighbor [Sefer Qorri] was told to leave the house and he was also told to walk in the same direction, and at about the same point they shot him too.

After that many other houses were burned. Smoke was rising and it kept me from seeing but I saw two more silhouettes walking and falling but I could not see who it was.[34]

According to this witness, twenty-eight houses were burned and many were looted. This number was confirmed by Zahride Podrimçaku, an activist from Glogovac for the Council for the Defense of Human Rights and Freedoms, who witnessed the attack from her balcony about 500 meters away. According to her, twenty-nine houses were burned and she saw the police taking away television sets and video recorders.[35]

A woman from Novi Poklek, who was among the women and children taken into Sefer Qorri's house, largely corroborated the other witness' story. According to her, the police, who were familiar with Albanian customs, went from house to house ordering the men of the households to hand over their guns. She said:

One [policeman] approached us and said that the head of the household should come out. He said give me your gun. My husband said that he had no gun and that he only works for his

[34]Human Rights Watch interview, Vasiljevo, June 7, 1998.

[35]Human Rights Watch interview with Zahride Podrimçaku, Priština, June 9, 1998

family. He said just give it. "You have a good house, you are wealthy so it is not possible that you don't have a gun." He had green eyes and a thin gold chain. He was not tall and was dirty blond. He wore black gloves and was in a policeman's uniform. They told my husband to go on and take the weapon and they made the children and women go outside and lie down.

According to this woman, her husband emerged from the house with some policemen holding a cloth on his bleeding head. One policemen allegedly said, "How could you not have guns if you have this?" — waving an Albanian state flag. Another policemen then came and held a gun to her husband's mouth ordering him to lie down. Then they told all of them to walk to the house of Safit Qorri. She said:

All of us were told to go in the house and we were led to a room. When we entered there was a guy watching us and he spoke Serbian and Albanian. There were ten men and fifty or sixty women. They asked the men where their sons were. One old man didn't understand Serbian and they hit him. One policeman pulled out his knife and threatened him saying, "I'll show you now." My husband said to the police "In God's name, don't do it." The policeman stopped and said I'll leave you alone, but you'll see what happens when Lutka[36] comes.

Another guy then came with a green uniform. He had black gloves and a black vest with thinning, short blond hair. He told the other policemen to separate the men and the women. He asked my husband where he is from. The men were in the other room but I heard him say he is from Vasiljevo, so he decided to send us [the women and children] in that direction. We went outside and they ordered us to walk and not to stop. When we started to walk we heard shooting. We were running and bullets were flying all around, even at us, so we kept going. The men were still in the house.[37]

---

[36]"Lutka" means "doll" in Serbian.

[37]Human Rights Watch interview, Vasiljevo, June 7, 1998.

Zahride Podrimçaku was in Novi Poklek on June 1 and saw the body of Ardian Deliu with a bullet wound in his left cheek and one in the left side of his neck. She told Human Rights Watch that she saw nine spots of blood, and shoes, a belt, and coat buttons near the blood marks.[38] Human Rights Watch spoke with two foreign journalists who were in Novi Poklek that week. Carsten Ingemann, a Danish photographer, said:

> I saw several blood stains on the ground. They looked similar.
> In some of the places you could see that there was shooting there
> because there were holes in the ground. I saw three or four
> blood splotches. One was from the same person. You could see
> the blood spot and then a trail of blood, like the body had been
> dragged, and then another blood spot with a bullet hole in the
> ground.[39]

An American journalist, Philip Smucker, was also in Novi Poklek that week. He told Human Rights Watch that he saw blood in eight places in the area where villagers said the men had been shot, as well as bullet casings next to the blood stains.[40]

What remains unclear in the Novi Poklek attack is whether the police faced any resistance from the Albanians prior to the concentration of villagers in Safit Qorri's house. One villager claimed that she saw a dead policeman and heard the police speaking on a walkie-talkie that one policeman had been killed. But she, like all the other villagers interviewed by Human Rights Watch, strenuously asserted that "there was no resistance."

All evidence points to at least one summary execution after police gathered Novi Poklek's villagers together, that of Ardian Deliu, and the detention and possible execution of nine others. As of September 1998, the police had not offered any information about the nine men last seen being taken away by the

---

[38]Human Rights Watch interview with Zahride Podrimçaku, Priština, June 9, 1998.

[39]Human Rights Watch interview with Carsten Ingemann, Priština, June 7, 1998.

[40]Human Rights Watch interview with Philip Smucker, Priština, June 7, 1998. See also Philip Smucker, "Villagers Tell of Ouster, Mass Executions," *The Washington Times*, June 5, 1998, and Tim Butcher, "Hidden Massacre is Uncovered in Kosovo Village," *Sunday Telegraph*, June 28, 1998.

police, despite requests from the families and their lawyers.[41] The nine missing are: Ahmet Berisha (40), Hajriz Hajdini (48), Muhamet Hajdini (45), Sahit Qorri (60), Sefer Qorri, (55), Ferat Hoti (39), Rama Asllani (60), Fidel Berisha (17), and Blerim Shishani (15).

Villagers told Human Rights Watch that one man from the army in a military camouflage uniform was leading the action, while the others were in police uniforms. One villager said that the leader was about 165 cm. tall, well-built, and had short, blond hair and a reddish face. The name of Lutka, reportedly the vice-commander of the Glogovac police station, was also mentioned a number of times as someone who was present. Some villagers also claim that they saw Pero Damjarac, the police chief in Glogovac, entering the village in a white Volkswagen during the action.

Zahrije Podrimçaku, an activist for the Council for Defense of Human Rights and Freedoms who investigated the incident, was arrested by the police in Priština on June 9, 1998, about one hour after she told Human Rights Watch about her findings in Novi Poklek. On June 13 she was charged with "terrorist acts," according to Articles 125 and 136 of the Yugoslav Penal Code, and is currently in the Lipljan prison. According to her lawyer, Liria Osmani, Podrimçaku has been subjected to some physical abuse while in detention.[42] (See section on Detentions and Arrests.)

---

[41]Letter submitted to the district court in Priština by the lawyers Fazli Balaj, Bajram Kelmendi, Destan Rukiqi, Lirije Osmani, and Nekibe Kelmendi, June 11, 1998.

[42]Human Rights Watch interview with Liria Osmani, Priština, October 1, 1998.

4. VIOLATIONS IN THE YUGOSLAV-ALBANIA BORDER REGION

After a period of intense shuttle diplomacy by American diplomat Richard Holbrooke, on May 15, 1998, Yugoslav President Slobodan Milošević met the ethnic Albanian leader Ibrahim Rugova for the first time in almost ten years. The talks were heralded by Western governments as "a positive first step" that could lead to a negotiated settlement of the conflict. On May 25, the E.U. member states rewarded Milošević by deciding not to go forward with an earlier decision to impose a ban on investment in Serbia. (See section on Response of the International Community.)

That week, the Serbian police together with forces of the Yugoslav Army began the largest offensive to date against a series of villages on Kosovo's border with Albania. The offensive was apparently intended to create a cordon sanitaire along the border in order to cut off the supply routes of the UÇK. Up until that point, small arms and new recruits had been arriving in large numbers from northern Albania, a region that is largely out of the control of the Albanian government.

While UÇK troops were definitely in the area, and at times were attacking the police and army, many villages from Peć in the north to Đakovica in the south were shelled while civilians were still present. Noncombatants who fled the attacks were sometimes fired on by snipers, and a still undetermined number of people were taken into detention. Afterwards, most villages in the region were systematically destroyed, and farmers' livestock was shot, to ensure that no one could return in the short run. Human Rights Watch conducted an investigation in the area in September and saw clear indications that houses had been set on fire where there was no evidence that combat had occurred.

The offensive was clearly intended to depopulate the region. Approximately 15,000 people fled over the mountains into Albania, sometimes under fire from the police and army, and an estimated 30,000 escaped northwards into Montenegro. An unknown number went east towards the then-UÇK held territory in Drenica.

Human Rights Watch spent four days interviewing refugees in northern Albania and Tirana, Albania's capital, in late June, and two weeks interviewing refugees in Montenegro in September. A clear pattern emerged of detentions, beatings, indiscriminate shelling, excessive force, and the systematic destruction of villages. One refugee claimed to have witnessed the rape of six people, two of them thirteen-year-old girls. On three occasions, refugees said, helicopters marked with the red cross fired on refugees heading for the border.[43]

Based on interviews with refugees in Albania, Human Rights Watch heard of shelling in the following villages and towns: Dečan, Junik, Bakaj, Bokež, Carabreć, Prilep, Ljocan, Vokša, Drenovac, Slup, Dobroš, Rastevica, Ljubuša, Nivokaz, Ponoševac, Poberž, Smolic, Jasić, Isnić, Strelc, Polać, and Polluž.

Use of Indiscriminate Force and Attacks on Civilians

Refugees interviewed by Human Rights Watch in Albania and Montenegro told strikingly similar stories about the shelling of their villages. Most often the attacks began in the early morning, around 5:00 a.m., without warning. The villagers would flee into the woods or the mountains until the shelling subsided. Many civilians were reportedly killed during the shelling and as they attempted to flee their villages.

Civilians, predominantly women, children, and elderly people, would travel from village to village, sometimes under the escort of armed male family members or the UÇK. When there was no place left to go, they crossed the mountains into Albania. Along the way, the police or army sometimes fired in their direction, and occasionally at them directly.

Shkurta Bacaj from Drenovac said she left her village on May 25 and went to her uncle's home in Junik because they were shelling:

> At 7 a.m. they began [shelling] and it went on all day. In the evening we left the village. When they shelled, every person in the village went to a village where they had family. We had no other solution but to go to the mountain. The place where they shell from is Hulaj village, where the police are based. They shell from there and we had to be careful because the police were shooting at us too. We were lots of children, old women and men.[44]

---

[43]See also a report by Physicians for Human Rights based on a mission to northern Albania in June. The report documents "serious human rights violations, including detentions, arbitrary arrests, violent beatings and rape, throughout Kosovo during the past six months." Physicians for Human Rights, "Medical Group Recounts Individual Testimony of Human Rights Abuses in Kosovo," June 24, 1998.

[44]Human Rights Watch interview with Shkurta Bacaj, Bajram Curri, Albania, June 16, 1998.

She and her family stayed four days in Junik, until the shelling began there too on May 30.

According to Ms. Bacaj, everybody in Junik left the village, in total some 7,000 Junik inhabitants and 5,000 people who had come to Junik from nearby villages. Ms. Bacaj went to Dobroš. Along the way, snipers injured her grandmother, Time Gazheraj, and six others, including Hate Shalaj, who later died, Caush Cestaj, Osman Gazheraj, and Shkelzen Kukaj. Then Ms. Bacaj herself was injured. She told Human Rights Watch:

> While I was walking they saw us and they shot at us in order to kill. The police shot at us and hit me in the leg. We lay down on the ground, then they kept on shooting. The bullet entered my left leg and right arm. We were a group of eight [her father, two sisters, a niece, younger brother and two uncles]. Only I was hit. We stayed there [in a ditch at a place called Shkoze] for fifteen hours not daring to move because they were shooting. From 7 a.m. to 10 p.m. we didn't dare to move. We returned to Junik when it got dark. Then they took me by car to Dobrosh, where I stayed for ten days.

Ms. Bacaj walked twelve hours through the mountains into Albania on June 9 without incident. Human Rights Watch visited her in the Bajram Curri hospital and saw two bullet scars. One bullet apparently entered her lower left shin and exited above the knee; the other bullet grazed the right shoulder.

Other refugees said that they were shot at as they tried to cross the border. Human Rights Watch interviewed the Selmanaj family just as they arrived in Bajram Curri directly from the mountains. Two women and one man escorted ten children, ranging in age from a baby to twelve years old. The children and the adults looked worn and dazed, having just walked for two days and two nights through the mountains. One of the women said:

> We left my village [Rastavica] three months ago when there was the attack on Glodjane. We have been moving for three months. Two nights ago we left and we have been traveling for two days and two nights. In the night they tried to shoot us. They were

shelling us in the forest. They put lights on us and fired. They were shooting at us with helicopters near the border.[45]

One woman from the village of Slup said:

We left Jasic at 6 a.m. for the border. We were lucky that no one shot at us. While we were coming, an airplane came and was shooting. An airplane was following us and bombing. We were 300 people all spread out. They shot with automatic guns and bombs. They shot for two hours near the border. We hid in some caves. I don't know if there were injured people because we all hid in the caves.[46]

On June 21, Human Rights Watch interviewed Dr. Imra Vishi, a doctor from Kosovo who was working in the Bajram Curri hospital. He said that, since the refugees began arriving in early June, the hospital had treated twenty-two refugees in the department of surgery with gunshot wounds, shrapnel, or other similar injuries. Eight people with gunshot wounds were in the hospital at that moment, one of them, a twenty-three-year-old man, with multiple wounds believed to have been from a single projectile in Smolić on June 8.[47] According to Dr. Vishi, most of the twenty-two injuries since June 1 were incurred during the shelling of villages, but some people, he said, were injured in battle. Two people were injured by grenades while trying to cross the border. Human Rights Watch interviewed one seventy-year-old woman in the hospital, Time Maserekaj from Voks, who had bullet wound scars on her right forearm and left wrist from what she claimed was sniper fire.[48]

---

[45]Human Rights Watch interview with members of the Selmanaj family, Bajram Curri, Albania, June 19, 1998.

[46]Human Rights Watch interview with man from Slup, Bajram Curri, Albania, June 21, 1998.

[47]Dr. Vishi said that the patient had eight shrapnel-like wounds but claimed he had been struck by only one bullet.

[48]Human Rights Watch interview with Dr. Imra Vishi, Bajram Curri, Albania, June 21, 1998.

Some of the wounded interviewed were most likely injured while fighting with the police and army; as combatants, they do not have protected status under international humanitarian law unless hors de combat. However, noncombatants too were systematically attacked in their villages during indiscriminate shelling or deliberately targeted as they were fleeing. Common Article 3 of the Geneva Conventions clearly states that, in internal armed conflicts, civilians and others who have ceased to be combatants are protected persons who must be treated humanely, with specific prohibitions on murder, torture, or cruel, humiliating or degrading treatment. In addition, there is clear evidence that livestock was killed and villages were destroyed beyond any possible military need, which is also a violation of the rules of war (see section Legal Standards and the Kosovo Conflict).

Finally, refugees reported three incidents where helicopters marked with the Red Cross emblem fired on civilians. Two cases were reported by journalist Roy Gutman in an article published on June 22, 1998, in *Newsday*. Mr. Gutman told Human Rights Watch that he had spoken with four individuals who described observing a Red Cross helicopter firing on people near Rrasa e Zogut (in Albanian) on June 13 and 14. He also spoke with one witness who said he saw the same thing at Baba i Bokes (in Albanian) on June 11.[49]

Human Rights Watch interviewed one witness who claimed to have seen a Red Cross helicopter engaged in military activity: this, however, was a UÇK soldier who said that the helicopter fired on civilians in Smolić on approximately June 2, 1998.[50]

Summary Executions in Ljubenić

There is still no clear picture of what happened in Ljubenić on May 25, 1998. But interviews with six witnesses conducted by six different organizations suggest that at least eight ethnic Albanians were executed by the Serbian special police.

The first account of the executions was made by the Kosova Information Center (KIC), a news service close to Ibrahim Rugova's Democratic League of Kosovo. In its May 26 bulletin, KIC reported that police killed the following nine people in Ljubenić: Zeqe Hamzaj (68), Brahim Hamzaj (64), Dervish Hamzaj (51), Ymer Hamzaj (53), Gani Hamzaj (25), Rifat Hamzaj (24), Bashkim Hamzaj (23),

---

[49]Human Rights Watch interview with Roy Gutman, Bajram Curri, Albania, June 21, 1998.

[50]Human Rights Watch interview with UÇK soldier, Tirana, Albania, June 23, 1998.

Hysen Alimehaj (40), and Haxhi Goga (24). One eye witness, Mehmet Gogaj, reportedly told KIC:

> Around 1:15 p.m., the Serb army started shelling Albanian homes. A bit later, many policemen in buses and armored personnel carriers surrounded the Ljubenic village. The Serb forces raided houses of local Albanians, killing and massacring people. Men were forced out in the yards and executed in front of their family members. The Serbs also took my three sons and my nephew. They were forced to stand against the outside wall of the house. Then, the Serbs walked several meters back and started firing rallies from automatic rifle on them. The four boys fell to the ground. There was nothing I could do.[51]

Two human rights organizations, the Humanitarian Law Center and Amnesty International, subsequently interviewed witnesses who had slightly different stories, but were able to confirm some executions. According to the Amnesty International report on the incident, a civilian car possibly carrying reserve policemen was fired upon on the road between Dečan and Peć near Ljubenić on the morning of May 25. Ostensibly in retaliation, police with armored cars attacked Ljubenić from a distance with artillery for thirty minutes and then entered the village around 1:30 p.m. A group of police reportedly entered one house where fourteen people were sheltered and separated the men from the women and children. The women and children were told to run away, while the men were beaten. The men were then also ordered to run away and, as they were running, they were shot in the back. Ymer Hamzaj, Brahim Hamzaj, and Bashkim Hamzaj were killed; one man was injured but survived.

According to Amnesty International, a group of policemen also entered the house of Zeqe Hamzaj, who was taken away with his sons, Gani and Rifat. The three, together with a guest, Haxhi Goga (24), were reportedly told to strip to their underwear, beaten and then killed.[52]

The Helsinki Committee for Human Rights in Serbia interviewed one witness from Ljubenić, identified as N.N., who arrived in Plav, Montenegro, on June 3, 1998, with six other men. He told the Helsinki Committee that he saw the

---

[51]KIC, May 26, 1998.

[52]Amnesty International, "A Human Rights Crisis in Kosovo Province, Document Series A: Events to June 1998, #5: Ljubenić and Poklek: A Pattern Repeated," July 1998.

police kill nine of his neighbors, aged twenty-three to sixty-five, in front of their house, although no names were provided.[53]

Finally, the Council for the Defense of Human Rights and Freedoms interviewed Ardeshir Gogaj, who was wounded by the police in Ljubenić. He told the council:

> At about 12:30 p.m., after several shots, we saw the Serbian army and police from Peja [Peć] heading for Deçan [Dečan]. They entered the village of Ljubenić and beat women, children, elderly, and adults. Then they went into the house of Shaban Husku, where ten citizens from Deçan had hidden. They took women and children and lined them up to execute them. We could see what the Serbian army was doing to them. They came and took us out into the yard. They lined us up to execute us and opened fire towards us. My brother Haxhi Mehmet Goga was killed, whereas I was wounded. Later on, I went towards the place called "Zagerlla", where I saw many killed, about twenty-nine. On the way to the mosque, I saw many killed and wounded near the house of Rame Huskaj. I saw that Zeqe Misini and his two sons were killed. As I was wounded, I could not go further, so I went back home where my brother's corpse was. Then I passed out and I have no idea what happened later on. Once again, I point out that I have seen tens of killed and wounded who remained in the fields, as well as tens of houses that were ruined and burned. Our village has become ruins.[54]

In northern Albania, Human Rights Watch interviewed a refugee, T.H., from the village of Slup who had been in Ljubenić for four days prior to the morning of the attack, and gave a slightly different account of the attack. She said that police dressed in blue uniforms arrived in Ljubenić around 4:00 a.m. wearing masks. She told Human Rights Watch that she watched from a house about twenty meters away where she was staying with her three children:

---

[53]Helsinki Committee for Human Rights in Serbia, "Report on Refugees from Kosovo Situated in Montenegro," Belgrade, June 18, 1998.

[54]Council for the Defense of Human Rights and Freedoms, "Human Rights Violations in the Course of June-July 1998."

Four policemen came around 4:00 a.m. They wore masks. We were in the basement of M.D.'s house.... I saw from the window. The police took nineteen people from a house. It was three men, four woman and twelve children. They took an old man with twin daughters, thirteen years old. They pushed the old man against the wall of the garden. They took off the girls' clothes and four policemen raped the two daughters. . . It was all between 4:00 and 6:00 a.m..[55]

T.H. claimed to have seen the police shoot those in the yard, but Human Rights Watch was unable to confirm her account. However, taken together with the testimonies collected by the other human rights groups, the evidence is overwhelming that at least nine summary executions took place. Human Rights Watch also saw a photograph, allegedly of the Hamzaj family, which showed the bodies of four older men, ranging in age from forty to sixty, all of them in their underwear on the ground with bullet wounds to their bodies.

---

[55]Human Rights Watch interview with woman from Slop, Markaj, Albania, June 19, 1998.

5. THE USE OF LANDMINES

The Federal Republic of Yugoslavia has not signed the Convention on the Prohibition of the Use, Stockpiling, Production and Transfer of Anti-Personnel Mines and On their Destruction, known as the 1997 Mine Ban Treaty. At a regional conference on the treaty held in March 1998, the Yugoslav Ministry of Defense defended the decision by arguing that, "through no fault of her own," Yugoslavia had been, "excluded from the work of a number of international organizations, and been subjected to additional political, economic, and psychological pressure."[56]

---

[56]Basic Points of the Statement by the Representative of the Federal Republic of Yugoslavia at the International Seminar on Anti-Personnel Mines, Budapest, March 26-28, 1998. The Yugoslav government's justifications for not signing the landmines treaty are worth noting. At the regional seminar, the Yugoslav delegate said:

(I) Through no fault of her own, the Federal Republic of Yugoslavia has been, for a longer period in a very specific international situation, excluded from the work of a number of international organizations, and been subjected to additional political, economic, and psychological pressure, (II) It is evident that due to the above the Federal Republic of Yugoslavia has failed to participate in the process from the outset, therefore she has been unable to participate in the negotiations on the elaboration of the Convention's text on equal footing with other states, (III) During last year's second semester, over a period of accelerated work to prepare the Convention for signing, the Federal Republic of Yugoslavia was engaged with other priorities, in particular, in striving to contribute to the strengthening of the region's stability, coming to terms with the Dayton Agreement, then to successfully implement her obligations under the Agreement on the sub-regional control of armaments, to integrate herself in the institutions of the international community, and last by not least, to solve the humanitarian and social problems of refugees and to ameliorate the consequences of the war in her neighborhood, (IV) The experience we have gained in the course of implementing the obligations under the Agreement on the sub-regional control of armaments shows that - despite certain difficulties and being without any outside assistance - the Federal Republic of Yugoslavia can bear the costs related to the destruction of mines, and she can honor other financial obligations deriving from the Convention, too, (V) By maintaining her stock of anti-personnel mines for a certain period the Federal Republic of Yugoslavia does not threaten anybody, she does not use the mines, does not develop them, neither does she distribute, no export them to other countries but rather uses them for educational purposes in a very restricted way, primarily in teaching de-mining

The FRY representative to the seminar told the delegates that Yugoslavia was maintaining its stock of landmines only for the purposes of training. He said:

> By maintaining her stock of anti-personnel mines for a certain period, the Federal Republic of Yugoslavia does not threaten anybody, she does not use the mines, does not develop them, neither does she distribute, nor export them to other countries but rather uses them for educational purposes in a very restricted way, primarily in teaching de-mining techniques.[57]

Despite this, the United Nations, through information from the Kosovo Diplomatic Observer Mission (KDOM), has confirmed that either the Serbian police or the Yugoslav Army has placed anti-personnel and anti-tank mines on Yugoslavia's borders with Albania in the west and Macedonia in the south, as well as in some places in central Kosovo.

An August 25, 1998, a security alert issued by UNICEF said:

> While the United Nations High Commissioner for Refugees (UNHCR) cannot confirm various reports about mines in Kosovo, it is confirmed that mines have been laid along the Albanian and Macedonian border with Kosovo and in the areas of Lapusnik, Iglrevo, Rakovina and the road between Rakovina and Klina. Landmines are confirmed in the areas of:
>
> - Junik and surroundings, particularly a dirt road which goes to the north from the village of Junik
> - Yugoslav-Albanian border
> - South of Grevnik (south of Dolac checkpoint in Klina municipality)
> - Southwest of Komorane.[58]

According to the Anti-mining Friends Committee/Shoqata Anti-Mina, the Albanian branch of the International Campaign to Ban Landmines, approximately

---

techniques.

[57]Ibid.

[58]UNICEF, Security Alert: Landmine Information on Kosovo, August 25, 1998.

twenty refugees, including some UÇK fighters, arrived in a hospital in Tirana, Albania, with wounds from landmines around July 18, 1998. Most had fled Kosovo after the police overran the border town of Junik, which had been a stronghold of the UÇK. Those still in the hospital on August 1 told a member of the Anti-mining Friends Committee that they knew of eleven deaths from landmines in the villages of Ponashec, Mulliq and Rrasa e Zogut (all in Albanian), but Human Rights Watch was not able to confirm these cases.[59]

On August 20, 1998, U.S. State Department spokesman James Rubin accused Serbian forces of laying land mines around the town of Junik: "Reports indicate that the Serbs have mined paths around the village and refugees from the Junik area are entering Albania and have been treated for injuries consistent with anti-personnel land mines."[60]

According to the United Nations Preventive Deployment Force (UNPREDEP), the U.N. mission based in Macedonia, and the Macedonian Ministry of Defense, landmines have also been placed along the Yugoslav border with Macedonia, ostensibly to hinder the flow of arms into Kosovo, and possibly to deter any refugee outflow to Macedonia.[61] On August 5, an UNPREDEP spokesman said that the U.N. had spotted mines along the border and the Macedonian Ministry of Defense announced that mines had been placed near the Jazince and Blace border crossings.[62] The Macedonian media speculated whether the mines had been placed inside Macedonian territory, since the Macedonian and Yugoslav governments have not yet agreed on the exact location of their common border, which was an unmarked internal boundary until Macedonia gained its independence in 1991.

On August 5, the Anti-mining Friends Committee in Albania cited witnesses who had seen mines near five villages along the Yugoslav-Macedonia border: Gorance, Krivenik, Secishte, Dimce, and Dermja (in Albanian). According to the organization, signs marking landmine fields had been placed in these areas,

---

[59]Correspondence with Dhimiter Haxhimihali, August 1, 1998.

[60]U.S. State Department press briefing, Washington D.C., August 22, 1998.

[61]Milošević has, thus far, been careful not to destablize Macedonia, which is of strategic interest to the West.

[62]"Yugoslavia mines its border with Macedonia," Associated Press, August 5, 1998, and "Minefields near Jazince and Blace,"*Macedonian Information Center*, August 5, 1998.

and the Yugoslav Army had asked the local religious organizations to inform the local population of the mine fields.[63]

The first public and verifiable landmine incident occurred on September 14 when an armored car carrying a KDOM team from Canada and an Albanian translator hit an anti-tank mine on a road just south of Likovac in the Drenica region. The car flipped over but nobody was seriously hurt. On September 25, five Serbian policemen were killed when their car hit a landmine in the same area. Five days later, a non-armoured vehicle of the International Committee of the Red Cross (ICRC) also hit a mine in the area, killing one ethnic Albanian doctor, Shpetim Robaj, and wounding three others. Likovac used to be a base of the UÇK and it is suspected, but not proven, that the mines were planted by the Albanian insurgents.

---

[63]Letter from Besnik Alibali, head of the Anti-mining Friends Committee/Shoqata Anti-Mina, August 5, 1998.

6. FORCIBLE DISAPPEARANCES

Well over one hundred ethnic Albanians have "disappeared" in Kosovo since February 1998, approximately half of whom were last seen in the custody of the police. The precise number, however, is impossible to determine since the Yugoslav authorities do not make public the number of people they have in detention, despite requests from Human Rights Watch and other organizations, including the ICRC.[64] Some of the "disappeared" may be in prison, while others are in hiding, have fled Kosovo, or joined the UÇK; others may have been secretly executed.

The most comprehensive report on missing persons, both Albanians and Serbs, was published in August 1998 by the Humanitarian Law Center.[65] According to the center, 119 ethnic Albanians have "disappeared" in the Kosovo conflict. Forty-four of these "disappearances" are directly attributable to the police, while seventy-two occurred in unclear circumstances. The Humanitarian Law Center documented three cases of ethnic Albanians who were detained and held without acknowledgment by the UÇK; the actual number is believed to be much higher. The center also documented 112 cases of ethnic Serbs who are unaccounted for and may have been seized — or killed— by the UÇK. (See section on Abuses by the UÇK.)

Below are some cases of "disappearances" of ethnic Albanians believed to have been carried out by government forces:

Dr. Hafir Shala

On April 10, 1998, Dr. Hafir Shala, a doctor with the Health Care Center in Glogovac, was taken into detention by the police, along with two friends, Hetem Sinani and Shaban Neziri. The latter two were interrogated and released but Mr. Shala was held. He has not been seen or heard from since.

The three men were traveling in Shaban Neziri's car to Priština when the traffic police stopped the car near Slatina village around 8:00 a.m. As the police were checking their identification, three men in plain clothes emerged from a black jeep that was parked nearby and told Dr. Shala to come with them to Priština, while Mr. Sinani and Mr. Neziri were instructed to follow in their car. All three men

---

[64]Human Rights Watch letters to Yugoslav Minister of Internal Affairs Zoran Sikolovic and Yugoslav Minister of Justice Zoran Knežević, July 20, 1998.

[65]Humanitarian Law Center, "Disappearances in Times of Armed Conflict," Spotlight Report Number 27, August 5, 1998.

were taken to the police station in Priština and interrogated in separate rooms until 2:00 p.m.. At that time, Mr. Sinani and Mr. Neziri were released. They told their lawyer, Destan Rukiqi, that they heard Dr. Shala screaming from pain from an unknown room in the police station as they left.[66]

Mr. Rukiqi told Human Rights Watch that he had taken various measures to locate Dr. Shala, all to no avail. On April 16, he wrote to the Serbian Ministry of Justice, the Serbian Prosecutor's office, and the district prosecutor in Priština. The next day, the Priština prosecutor, Slavko Stevanovic, said the State Security office in Priština had no information on Shala's whereabouts. Letters written by Human Rights Watch to the Serbian and Yugoslav Ministries of Interior and Justice on July 20, 1998, asking for information on Dr. Shala's case remain unanswered.

Fourteen Members of the Jashari Family

Fourteen members of the Jashari family remained unaccounted for after the March 5 police attack on their family compound in Donji Prekaz (see section on Abuses in Drenica). Ten people were buried by the police on March 10 without proper identification, so it is possible that the missing Jashari family members are among those buried at that time.

Jakup Qerimi

According to the Council for the Defense of Human Rights and Freedoms, the police detained Jakup Qerimi, a twenty-seven-year-old ethnic Albanian who is mentally handicapped, in Uroševac on June 20, and he has not been seen since. The police allegedly told his mother that she would never see her son again.

Idriz Idrizi

According the Council for the Defense of Human Rights and Freedoms and the Humanitarian Law Center, Idriz Idrizi from Srbica was taken by the police on January 23 from near the ammunition factory outside of Donji Prekaz. As of September 1998, he was still unaccounted for.[67] (See section on Abuses in Drenica.)

---

[66]Human Rights Watch interview with Destan Rukiqi, Priština, June 3, 1998.

[67]Spotlight Report Number 27, "Disappearances in Times of Armed Conflict," Humanitarian Law Center, August 5, 1998.

Nine Men from Novi Poklek

On May 31, 1998, Serbian special police forces attacked the village of Novi Poklek near Glogovac. Ten men were taken by the police: the body of one of them, Ardian Deliu, was found the next day. The other nine men are still "disappeared."

A witness told Human Rights Watch that he saw the police shoot five men dead, three of whom he identified as Sefer Qorri, Hajriz Hajdini, and Ahmet Berisha, although his account could not be confirmed by Human Rights Watch. (See section on Abuses in Drenica.) The nine missing men from Poklek are: Ahmet Berisha (40), Hajriz Hajdini (48), Muhamet Hajdini (45), Sahit Qorri (60), Sefer Qorri (55), Ferat Hoti (39), Rama Asllani (60), Fidel Berisha (17), and Blerim Shishani (15).

7. DETENTIONS AND ARRESTS

Arbitrary detentions and arrests of ethnic Albanians have escalated rapidly throughout 1998. Until late September, the precise number of individuals in custody at any given time had been impossible to determine since the Yugoslav authorities refused to provide detailed information, despite specific inquiries from Human Rights Watch.[68] On October 4, Serbian Ministry of Justice stated that criminal investigations had been opened against 1,246 individuals in five local courts of Kosovo and one court in Prokupje—all of them on charges of terrorism or enemy activities against the state. According to the ministry, 684 of these people were in detention.[69]

In July and August, detained individuals increasingly included human rights activists, humanitarian aid workers, political party members, doctors, and lawyers, many of whom were physically abused in custody. Human Rights Watch has substantial and credible evidence from lawyers and family members of detainees that torture and ill-treatment of detainees is common, especially in the police stations during the first days in custody. From March to August 1998, five people are known to have died from torture while in police custody; hundreds of others have been beaten. Human rights and humanitarian agencies, including the International Committee of the Red Cross, report restricted access to detainees.[70]

According to the Yugoslav government, a round of trials will begin in October, and eight judges will be sent to Kosovo to deal with the high case load.[71] In the past, terrorism-related trials have been marred by serious procedural irregularities, as well as the use of torture to extract confessions.[72]

---

[68]Human Rights Watch letters to Yugoslav Minister of Internal Affairs Zoran Sikolovic and Yugoslav Minister of Justice Zoran Knežević, July 20, 1998.

[69]Beta, October 4, 1998.

[70]*ICRC Position on the Crisis in Kosovo,* International Committee of the Red Cross, September 1998.

[71]NT Plus, September 18, 1998.

[72]See Human Rights Watch/Helsinki, "Persecution Persists: Human Rights Violations in Kosovo," December 1996, and "Human Rights Watch/Helsinki Condemns Political Trial in Kosovo," Press Release, July 15, 1997. Yugoslav laws guarantees all defendants the right to due process. Article 23 of the federal constitution forbids arbitrary detention and obliges the authorities to inform a detainee immediately of the reason for his

Arrests

Regarding arrests, Human Rights Watch obtained the following general information:

• According to Adem Bajri, a prominent lawyer in Peć, as of September 21, 251 ethnic Albanians were in the Peć jail facing charges of terrorist activity. Criminal charges had been filed against 510 others who remain at large. Mr. Bajri told Human Rights Watch that he personally has twenty-four clients in prison, all of whom are facing charges of terrorism. Mr. Bajri has been allowed to visit his clients and said that virtually all of them show signs of torture, including injuries such as bruises on the body and broken bones.[73]

• On July 20 the police stopped a bus near Podujevo that was traveling to Kosovo from Slovenia. Fifty-four ethnic Albanians who had been working in Slovenia were initially arrested. On August 17, thirty-nine of them were released. Bajram Krasniqi, a lawyer who visited them on July 29 in Prokuple prison, told Human Rights Watch that he saw clear signs that they had been beaten.[74] The other fifteen people remain in prison charged with terrorist acts based on Articles 125 and 136 of the Serbian Penal Code.[75] At the time of arrest, the police took from the accused a total of 352,018 DM.

• On May 23, eight students from the Pedagogical High School "Xhevdet Doda" in Prizren and one student from the University of Pristina, all of

_____

or her detention and to grant that person access to a lawyer. Article 24 obliges the authorities to inform the detainee in writing of the reason for his or her arrest within twenty-four hours. Detention ordered by a lower court may not exceed three months, unless extended by a higher court to a maximum of six months. Article 25 outlaws torture against a detainee, as well as any forcible extraction of confessions or statements. The use of force against a detainee is also a criminal offence.

[73]Human Rights Watch interview with Aden Bajri, Peć, September 21, 1998.

[74]Human Rights Watch interview with Bajram Krasniqi, September 19, 1998.

[75]Republic of Serbia Prosecutor's Office, Kt. Nr. 55/98, July 23, 1998, Prokuple, signed by District Prosecutor Miroslav Nikiolic.

them members of the Students' Independent Union, were arrested in Prizren. On June 8, they were charged with UÇK membership and committing terrorist acts. On August 24, they were convicted of "enemy activity" against the state because they had organized first aid courses in Prizren and sentenced to prison terms ranging from one to seven and a half years. Four of the students were also charged with having contacted the UÇK. The lawyer for some of the students, Hazër Susuri, told Human Rights Watch that two of his clients, Bylbyl Duraku and Sejdi Bullanica, had been beaten in pre-trial detention. According to Mr. Susuri and an international observer who monitored the trial, the entire proceedings for all nine students lasted four and a half hours. Their convictions were based entirely on the confessions they had made in detention. Their sentences were as follows:[76]

Nijazi Kryeziu (21)	seven and a half years in prison
Aqif Iljazi (21)	six and a half years in prison
Bylbyl Duraku (22)	five and a half years in prison
Sejdi Bellanica (23)	three and a half years in prison
Defrim Rifaj (22)	two and a half years in prison
Behare Tafallari (22)	two years in prison
Jehona Krasniqi (22)	two years in prison
Leonora Morina (21)	two years in prison
Sherif Iljazi (20)	one year in prison

•   According to the Serbian police, after intense fighting with the UÇK in Orahovac, the police arrested 223 ethnic Albanians suspected of "terrorism." All of the detained were released after questioning, except for twenty-six Albanians who remained in custody and are facing criminal charges.[77]

•   On September 4 and 5, the Serbian police detained more than 600 ethnic Albanians from around the villages of Ponorac, Ratkovac, and Drenovac

---

[76]Human Rights Watch Interview with Hazer Susuri in Prizren on September 21, 1998.

[77]United Nations Office of the High Commissioner for Human Rights, "Report from the Human Rights Field Operation in Bosnia and Hercegovina, the Republic of Croatia, and the Federal Republic of Yugoslavia," August 7, 1998.

who had been internally displaced because of fighting.[78] According to diplomatic sources who spoke with witnesses, the women and children were released and the men were taken to the Ponorac schoolhouse, where they were filmed by Serbian state television as "captured terrorists." Most of the men were reportedly released on September 5 but an estimated thirty-one people remained in police custody, nine of whom were released a few days later. Human Rights Watch saw photographs of the alleged "terrorists"which showed a large group of men on their knees with the hands behind their heads being guarded by armed police officers.

•   On September 24, the Media Center in Priština reported that, according to the police, 194 ethnic Albanians had been arrested on September 22 and 23 during a police action in the Čičavica Mountains northwest of Priština. The authorities have opened investigations against those arrested. In contrast, on September 26, the Albanian daily Koha Ditore cited Ministry of Interior spokesman Bozidar Filic as saying that 325 Albanians had been arrested.[79]

Some individual cases are outlined below:

Destan Rukiqi

Destan Rukiqi, a lawyer in Priština who has defended dozens of ethnic Albanian political prisoners in Kosovo in recent years, was arrested on July 23, 1998, and sentenced that same day in a summary proceeding to the maximum sixty days in prison for disturbing public order (under Article 6, paragraph 3 of the Serbian Law on Public Order). The arrest was related to an incident that morning, when Rukiqi had raised his voice at a district judge in Priština, Ms. Danica Marinković,[80] telling her, "I am in the court but you are acting like the police," after

---

[78]Ljubomir Milasin, "Hundreds of Kosovars Detained, UNHCR Warns of Bosnia Spectre," AFP, September 8, 1998, and Tanjug, September 6, 1998.

[79]Koha Ditore, "PB e Serbise: Ka perfunduar aksioni ne Qyqavice, jane arrestuar 325 shqiptare," September 26, 1998.

[80]Judge Marinkovic has presided over a number of political trials against ethnic Albanians in Kosovo in which the defendants were tortured. See Human Rights Watch/Helsinki, "Persecution Persists: Human Rights Violations in Kosovo," December 1996, pg 22.

she had refused to let Rukiqi take notes while reviewing the case file of his client, Cen Dugolli (see below).

Mr. Rukiqi was severely beaten on his third day in detention by policemen at the Priština prison. He told Human Rights Watch that he was held down and beaten on his hands, feet and kidneys with a three-foot long rubber baton. Over the next two weeks, he underwent dialysis eleven times.[81] Mr. Rukiqi's sentence was reduced by the Serbian Supreme Court to thirty days, and he was released on August 22.

Rukiqi had been involved in a number of human rights related cases, and he had provided information on war crimes committed by Serbian special police forces in Kosovo to the war crimes tribunal in the Hague.

Zahride Podrimçaku

Ms. Zahrida Podrimçaku, an activist with the Council for the Defense of Human Rights and Freedoms in Glogovac, was detained by police in Priština on June 8, 1998, together with Ibrahim Makolli, who works at the council's offices in Priština.[82] Mr. Makolli was released after a few hours of questioning, but Ms. Podrimçaku remained in custody and was denied contact with a lawyer or her family for several days. On September 8, she was charged with committing "terrorist acts" (Articles 125 and 136 of the Serbian Penal Code) for allegedly having transported military goods, including an automatic weapon, to an UÇK commander in Drenica. Podrimçaku's lawyer, Liria Osmani, told Human Rights Watch that she saw signs of physical abuse on Ms. Podrimçaku during her first visit to Lipljan prison on June 19 and again on August 12.[83] Podrimçaku is awaiting trial but, as of October 1, no court date had been set.

Ms. Podrimçaku had been investigating what happened on May 31, 1998, in the village of Novi Poklek, when police detained ten ethnic Albanian men during an attack on the village. The body of one of the men, Ardian Deliu, was found the next day, while the other nine men remain missing and are presumed dead. (See section on Abuses in Drenica.)

---

[81]Human Rights Watch telephone interview with Destan Rukiqi, August 23, 1998.

[82]Podrimcaku's arrest occurred about one hour after she had spoken with a Human Rights Watch researcher about her investigations in Novi Poklek.

[83]Human Rights Watch interview with Liria Osmani, Priština, October 1, 1998.

Besa Arllati

Ms. Besa Arllati, chairwoman of the LDK information commission in Đakovica, was arrested on May 26 and brought to the police station in Đakovica, where she was interrogated and beaten by police chief Sreten Ćamatović.[84] The police reportedly wanted to know about two Serbian policemen, Nikola Jovanović and Rade Popadić, who they believed had been seized by the UÇK. Arllati was detained and interrogated on and off for the next few days, until June 1, about the work of the UÇK and the activities of Albanians in the area.

Dr. Fehmi Vula

Dr. Fehmi Vula, a surgeon at the Đakovica hospital, member of the Đakovica LDK presidency and member of the shadow Kosovo Parliament, was arrested on May 29, 1998. On June 3, a Prizren court extended his detention to thirty days to investigate possible "terrorist acts" as defined in Article 136 of the Serbian penal code. As of September 1, Dr. Vula was in detention awaiting trial.

Mevlude Sarraqi

Mrs. Mevlude Sarraqi, member of the LDK presidency, head of the LDK Women's Forum, and a member of the Kosovo Parliament, was arrested on June 1 in Đakovica and charged with "Association for the purpose of hostile activity" under Article 136 of the Serbian penal code. She was arrested in advance of a rally organized by the Women's Forum to protest the detention of LDK activists, such as Dr. Vula and Besa Arllati. According to her lawyer, Liria Osmani, Ms. Sarraqi was held for four days in the state security buidling in Đakovica, where she was beaten. As of October 1 she was in Lipljan womens prison awaiting trail.[85]

Deaths in Detention

Cen Dugolli

Cen Dugolli, an activist with the Democratic League of Kosovo in Uroševac, died on August 17, 1998, in Priština Hospital from beatings sustained while in detention. According to his family, the police arrested Cen and his neighbor, Haxhi Bytyqi, at 8:00 a.m. on June 21, 1998, from their homes in Uroševac. Cen was taken to the Gnjilane prison a few days later and then

---

[84]Humanitarian Law Center, "Kosovo - Disappearances in Times of Armed Conflict," Spotlight Report No. 27, August 5, 1998.

[85]Human Rights Watch interview with Liria Osmani, Priština, October 1, 1998.

transferred to the Priština prison. He was taken by police to the Priština hospital on August 16 and died the next day from internal injuries, according to the official autopsy report seen by Human Rights Watch.

Dugolli's family told Human Rights Watch that they first visited Cen on July 1 in Priština prison and that he showed signs of physical abuse, such as bruises on the face. The family was supposed to visit Cen on August 17 but was not allowed in by the prison guards. That night they learned from the Albanian satellite television news from Albania that Cen had died.[86] Human Rights Watch saw photographs of Mr. Dugolli that showed severe signs of torture, including deep bruising that covered large parts of his body.

Dugolli's lawyer, Destan Rukiqi, was arrested on July 23 for "insulting" Judge Danica Marinković while trying to review Dugolli's case file. Rukiqi himself spent thirty days in prison and was severely beaten on the kidneys while in the Lipljan prison (see above).

Rexhep Bislimi

Rexhep Bislimi, an activist with the Council for the Defense of Human Rights and Freedoms in Uroševac was arrested on July 6, 1998, from the street in Uroševac, and died on July 22 from beatings he sustained while in detention. According to Bislimi's family, the police brought Rexhep back to his house on July 7 and made him dig some holes in the garden to look for weapons they thought he had hidden there, but they found nothing. Members of the family told Human Rights Watch that Rexhep had bruises on his face, as well as blood.[87] Three days later, the family learned that Rexhep was in Gnjilane prison, but they were never allowed to see him. On July 19, the family learned that Rexhep had been taken to the Priština hospital, but they were again not able to see him because two policemen were guarding his hospital room. Rexhep died on July 21 due to, according to the official autopsy report, "constusio capitis et corporis." Human Rights Watch saw a photograph of Mr. Bislimi that showed severe bruising on large sections of his legs and torso that were consistent with allegations of torture.

---

[86]Human Rights Watch interview with the Dugolli family, Uroševac, September 25, 1998.

[87]Human Rights Watch interview with the Bislimi family, Uroševac, September 25, 1998.

Adem Berisha

According to the Council for the Defense of Human Rights and Freedoms, Adem Berisha from Bruc village, died on August 18, 1998, in the Prizren hospital reportedly from injuries inflicted by police during his detention in Prizren. He had been arrested on the Dragas-Prizren road on August 16.

Bilall Shala

According to Albanian media reports, on August 29, around 11:00 p.m., forty-seven-year-old Bilall Shala from Uroševac died while in police custody. Shala was arrested in Uroševac on August 28 together with his son, Agron, who was released later that day, reportedly after having been beaten by the police. Bilall's brother, Zenel Shala, told the Albanian media that he was informed on the evening of August 28 that his brother had died and was in the Priština city morgue.[88]

Maksut Qafleshi

According to the Council for the Defense of Human Rights and Freedoms, on August 23 Maksut Qafleshi from Belobrade died as a result of police torture he sustained in Uroševac.[89] Maksut's brother told the Council that Maksut was arrested and beaten by the police on the road between Prizren and Uroševac, and was then taken to the police station in Uroševac, where he was denied medical treatment. He was later transferred to the hospital in Priština, where he died.

---

[88]"One More Albanian Dead From Prison Torture," Arta, August 30, 1998, and "Another Albanian Detainee Dies of Police Torture," KIC, August 30, 1998.

[89]"Within Two Months Five Albanians Die in Serbian Prisons," Council for the Defense of Human Rights and Freedoms, September 1998.

8. ATTACKS AND RESTRICTIONS ON MEDICAL AND RELIEF PERSONNEL

By September 1998, at least 300,000 people had been displaced in Kosovo, the vast majority of them ethnic Albanians. According to the United Nations High Commissioner for Refugees (UNHCR), as of August 31, 40,000 ethnic Albanians from Kosovo were in Montenegro, 15,000 were in Albania, and 20,000 were in Macedonia. An estimated 7,000 Albanians from Kosovo had even sought refuge in Bosnia.

Despite some returns, at least 35,000 displaced persons were considered "exposed" in mid-October, meaning they were without any shelter in the open mountains or woods. Humanitarian aid agencies and top government officials warn of a human catastrophe once winter arrives if shelter cannot be found for these people. U.S. Assistant Secretary of State for Population, Refugees, and Migration Julia Taft, who visited Kosovo in late August, said of her trip:

> It was one of the most heart-wrenching experiences I have had in twenty-five years of working in humanitarian relief. We have a catastrophe looming, and we only have as a world humanitarian community six weeks to help the government of Serbia respond to this crisis.[90] The snows come early, I understand, to this part of the world. With the snow may come the death of many of the more than 300,000 people who have been displaced from their homes because of the conflict in Kosovo.[91]

---

[90] Assistant Secretary of State Taft was referring to a proposal from the Yugoslav government to open eleven "humanitarian centers" around Kosovo to distribute aid to the internally displaced. On September 4, Assistant Administrator for Humanitarian Response at the U.S. Agency for International Development, Hugh Parmer, said that the U.S. government supports the Yugoslav government's idea and will donate U.S.$1.8 million for aid to displaced persons, in addition to the $11 million already provided. The money, Parmer said, would be used for emergency food packets to be distributed through the eleven centers announced by the Yugoslav government, but there was no clarification of the security measures that would guarantee the safety of the ethnic Albanians who came to receive aid.

[91] Press conference of Assistant Secretary of State Julia Taft, Belgrade, August 28, 1998.

Despite this, the Yugoslav government has posed a number of obstacles to the delivery of aid for internally displaced persons (IDPs), ignoring promises to allow unimpeded access for humanitarian agencies.[92] Moreover, it carried out a military offensive that resulted in further displacement and a security environment not conducive to return. Scattered in valleys and forests, many of the displaced are unreachable by the aid agencies working out of Priština. In addition, direct restrictions on the aid agencies, and even attacks, severely hinder their ability to reach those in need.

Albanian and foreign relief workers have faced a series of obstacles from the government in their attempts to deliver food to the internally displaced, including restricted access to needy populations, confiscation of supplies, harassment and, in the case of the Mother Theresa Society, the largest and most important local relief organization, occasional arrests and attacks.

The most serious attack on humanitarian aid workers, local or international, was the August 24 attack by Serbian police on an aid convoy that killed three ethnic Albanians working with the Mother Theresa Society. According to the *New York Times*, the August 24 attack occurred at mid-afternoon in an open field in the village of Vlaski Drenovac near Kijevo, when police fired upon an aid convoy of four tractors with cannon-fire from about half a mile away. The wagons were reportedly filled with boxes clearly marked "Doctors of the World," the relief agency that had donated the food supplies. According to the Mother Theresa Society, a direct hit on the second tractor killed Sadri Ramadan Gashi (65), Adem Isuf Morina (40), and Hajriz Haxhi Morina (25). A hit on the third tractor injured Mustafa and Habib Krasniqi. Local and international press, as well as the Mother Theresa Society, reported that the convoy had previously been allowed through a Serb checkpoint.[93] According to the *New York Times*, the government explained the barrage by saying that the police in an armored personnel carrier could not see what was in the wagons and became suspicious and opened fire. U.S. Department of State spokesman James Foley contradicted this by saying "the evidence indicates that the workers' vehicle was deliberately targeted by a Serbian armored vehicle

---

[92]Following a June 16, 1998, meeting between Presidents Milošević and Boris Yeltsin in Moscow, the Yugoslav government agreed, among other things, to allow diplomats and humanitarian agencies full access throughout Kosovo.

[93]*Arta*, Priština, Kosovo, August 24, 1998, and *The Guardian*, London, August 26, 1998.

less than a kilometer away in broad daylight."[94] Diplomats in Belgrade told Human Rights Watch that they were convinced the Serbian police had fired directly on the convoy from a nearby hill.[95]

In an August 28 press conference held in Priština after her brief visit to Kosovo, U.S. Assistant Secretary of State Julia Taft said she had raised the attack on the Mother Theresa Society convoy with the Yugoslav authorities. "I must say I was very reassured by the regret and the apology by the authorities that these people had been killed," she said. "And there is going to be an inspection."[96]

The incident was the second reported attack on Mother Theresa activists. On July 11, three men were fired upon by people believed to be the police while returning from an aid delivery in the village of Sibovac near Obilić. Xhevdet Stulçaku, vice president of the Mother Theresa Society in Obilić, was struck in the head with a bullet and is currently paralyzed on his right side of his body.[97] Selatin Hashani, secretary of the society in Obilić, was also wounded.

Also on July 11, two Mother Theresa Society activists in Đakovica, Fatime Boshnjaku and Uran Luxha, were arrested while delivering supplies in the nearby villages; Ms. Boshnjaku is currently in Lipljan womens prison awaiting trial on charges of assisting terrorists. Many other Mother Theresa activists have reported harassment and interrogations by the police.

On August 31, more than 200 ethnic Serb women demonstrated in front of the United States Information Agency office in Priština to protest reported executions of Serbian civilians by the UÇK in Klečka (see section on Abuses by the UÇK). They threw stones at the building shouting "Fascists!" and "Murderers!" as the police watched from a distance.[98] The crowd then moved to the office of the ICRC, where they pelted the building with stones and beat up an ethnic Albanian guard while accusing the ICRC of "bringing humanitarian aid to

---

[94]U.S. State Department Press Briefing, Washington D.C., August 27, 1998.

[95]Human Rights Watch interview, Belgrade, September 1, 1998.

[96]Press conference of U.S. Assistant Secretary Julia Taft, Priština, August 28, 1998.

[97] Human Rights Watch interview with Xhevdet Stulcaku in Obilić, September 22, 1998.

[98]"Serb Women Stone US Building In Protest; Yugoslavia Refuses Visa to US Envoy," AP, August 31, 1998.

the terrorists." According to one press report, the women then got on two buses that Serb policemen had brought for them.[99]

A fundamental problem for all humanitarian aid organizations working in Kosovo is restricted access to civilians in need. On numerous occasions, the Serbian police have blocked aid convoys on main roads. Some medical supplies and food stuffs have been confiscated by the police on the grounds that it was intended for "Albanian terrorists."

Human Rights Watch raised the issue of access with Boško Drobnjak, head of the Secretary of Information in Kosovo. He said that the police had occasionally blocked aid convoys because "some humanitarian organization have been helping terrorists. Not necessarily with weapons, but with military equipment."[100]

Humanitarian aid agencies working in Kosovo told Human Rights Watch that they are frequently denied access to areas where fighting is taking place. From May 20 to approximately June 21, for example, the ICRC was denied access to the Dečan area where a large police and army offensive was under way. An ICRC press release said that they had been denied access, "despite a number of previous assurances from the highest authorities in Belgrade that the ICRC would be able to work unhindered in Kosovo."[101]

In early July, the police forced an aid convoy from Medecins Sans Frontieres (MSF) to deliver its supplies to a collective center with ethnic Serbian refugees in Đakovica, rather than give it to the Mother Theresa Society for distribution, as MSF had intended.[102] On August 27, a Serbian police checkpoint at Slatina turned back an eight-truck convoy of the United Nations High Commissioner for Refugees (UNHCR) that was carrying one month's worth of food for more than 30,000 families.[103]

---

[99]"Serb Women Stone US Center, ICRC in Kosovo," AFP, August 31, 1998.

[100]Human Rights Watch interview with Boško Drobnjak, June 11, 1998, Priština.

[101]"Kosovo: ICRC Urgently Requests Access to Affected Areas," ICRC press release 98/21, June 3, 1998.

[102]Human Rights Watch interview with Francois Fille, Priština, June 10, 1998.

[103]"UNHCR Aid Convoy Repulsed Near Kosovo Capital Priština," AFP, August 27, 1998, and UN Inter-Agency Update on Kosovo, August 28, 1998.

The police also blocked aid deliveries during the police attacks in Drenica from February 28 to March 1. Doctors were also not allowed into the Drenica villages of Likošane, Ćirez and Prekaz to perform autopsies on those killed, although there was strong evidence to suggest summary executions (see section on Abuses in Drenica). In a press conference held on March 7 to explain the police actions in Drenica, Police Colonel Ljubinko Cvetić said that humanitarian organizations had been denied access to the area because some of them had supplied arms and equipment to terrorists.[104]

In August, international relief agencies reported continued obstructions by the government, such as the denial of visas for foreign staff, lengthy customs procedures for imported relief supplies, and the slow processing of licences for hand-held radios used by relief agencies to communicate with their staffs in the field.

The UÇK has reportedly also blocked some relief convoys (see section on Abuses by the UÇK).

---

[104]"Interior Ministry Spokesman Gives Press Conference," Tanjug, March 7, 1998.

9. GOVERNMENT RESTRICTIONS ON THE MEDIA

Since the armed conflict began in February 1998, the Yugoslav government has placed a number of serious restrictions on the work of local journalists, including threats, detentions, and beatings by the police. Independent radio and television stations in the Albanian language are denied broadcast licenses or, in one case, closed down.

The independent Serbian-language media is not exempt from state pressure. News wires, newspapers, and radio stations that report objectively on Kosovo are labeled "traitors" and threatened with legal action. In September, three newspapers were closed down because they violated a special government decree on the press that was passed in response to perceived NATO threats. As this report was going to print, the Serbian government had passed a highly restrictive Law on Public Information that banned foreign broadcasts of "a political-propaganda nature" and placed exceedingly high fines on violators of the law. As was the case during the wars in Bosnia and Croatia, the state-run radio and television purposefully spread disinformation about Kosovo and promoted images of "the enemy" intended to inflame the conflict.

The international media covering Kosovo also faces a number restrictions on its work, starting with the denial of visas to journalists the state considers critical of its policies. A number of foreign journalists have been beaten at demonstrations and fired upon by the police.

Restrictions on the Albanian-language Media

At least five ethnic Albanian journalists were beaten by the police in March 1998 during street demonstrations in Priština. On March 2, the police beat Veton Surroi, editor-in-chief of the daily *Koha Ditore*, Ibrahim Osmani, a journalist with Agence France Presse and the Voice of America, Avni Spahiu, editor-in-chief of the daily *Bujku*, Agron Bajrami, a journalist at *Koha Ditore*, and Sherif Kunjufca, a journalist with Albanian Television. Police forces also broke into the offices of *Koha Ditore* and beat people who had taken refuge inside; a photographer, Fatos Berisha, jumped from a second story window and broke his leg. Police also broke into the offices of *Bujku*.[105]

Since then, at least two other ethnic Albanian journalists have been beaten by the police. According to the *Koha Ditore* editorial offices in Priština, on August 19, five policemen in Đakovica entered the home of their local correspondent,

---

[105]Human Rights Watch interview with Agron Bajrami and Veton Surroi, Priština, May 22, 1998.

Musa Kurhasku, and confiscated articles, documents, his telephone book, and a telex machine. Kurhasku was reportedly ordered to the local police station where the police allegedly told him to go to another city, Orahovac, in order to negotiate the release of an ethnic Serb who had been captured by members of the UÇK. Mr. Kurhasku reportedly refused to go, saying that it was not a journalist's responsibility to act as a broker or to do the work of the Red Cross, and was beaten.[106] He has gone into hiding, as has another *Koha Ditore* correspondent, Adem Metaj, from Srbica.

On August 4, an editor with *Bujku*, Zeke Gecaj, was stopped by the police near the center of Priština. The police took Mr. Gecaj to the local station around 11:00 p.m. where he was questioned and told to report again the next morning. On August 5, he was interrogated for four hours and reportedly threatened.[107]

The Broadcast Media in Kosovo

The Yugoslav government does not allow any domestic independent radio or television stations to broadcast in Kosovo. Two start-up stations, Radio Koha and Radio 21 were denied frequency licenses in a public tender announced in February 1998. Radio 21 currently broadcasts over the Internet in Albanian and English (http://www.radio21.net).

Ethnic Albanians in Kosovo can receive the Albanian-language radio programs of the BBC, Deutsche Welle, and the Voice of America. A satellite television program from Tirana, Albania is also broadcast a few hours every day.

On July 1, 1998, the government shut down Radio Kontakt, an independent, multi-ethnic radio station in Kosovo, that strived, in its own words, to be a radio of "good-will and reconciliation" by providing objective news in both Albanian and Serbian. An inspector of the Yugoslav Telecommunications Ministry, accompanied by armed policemen in four police cars, entered the station's offices in Priština and confiscated part of the transmitter.[108]

---

[106]Although Human Rights Watch could not confirm this account, it is consistent with other reports of Serbian police ordering ethnic Albanian civilians to negotiate with the UÇK, such as the cases of Besa Arllati and Dr. Fehmi Vula, also from Đakovica.

[107]"IFJ Condemns Attacks on Journalists in Kosova," Press Release of the International Federation of Journalists, August 5, 1998, and "Bujku Editor in Serb Custody on Tuesday and Wednesday," KIC, August 4, 1998.

[108]IFEX Action Alert, July 7, 1998.

In a press conference on July 3 in Belgrade, Yugoslav Secretary of Information Goran Matic said that Radio Kontakt had been closed "because it did not tender in the competition for frequency allocation... this is a technical issue rather than a political one."[109] But Radio Kontakt had submitted all of the necessary documentation for the second round of the frequency tender and had received confirmation from the Ministry of Telecommunications that it would soon be granted a license. The station had been broadcasting only music during an experimental period beginning on June 19, 1998. The confiscation of its transmitter occurred two days after the station had begun rebroadcasting Radio B92, the BBC, and VOA.

Restriction on the Serbian-language Media

The Yugoslav government maintains direct control of the state radio and television, Radio Television Serbia (RTS), which provides news for the majority of the population. State programs blatantly glorify the government's accomplishments (real or imagined), conceal its failures and, most importantly, manipulate the fears of the ethnic Serbian population. During the fighting in Bosnia and Croatia, and now with war in Kosovo, state radio and television have purposefully spread disinformation and promoted an atmosphere of nationalist hysteria that has encouraged conflict.

Coupled with this is an ongoing attempt to hinder or make illegal the work of the private, independent media that has been struggling to break the information blockade. Conscious of the threat that objective news poses to its power, the Yugoslav government places various restrictions on Yugoslavia's independent newspapers, magazines, television and radio stations. Censorship is not blatant but is effectively applied through financial controls, legal manipulation, and police harassment.

Independent newspapers and magazines are faced with a host of problems, specifically restrictions on printing and distribution, both industries controlled by the state. Newspaper editors and journalists are sometimes subjected to harassment and, on occasion, physical violence by the police.

On March 6, 1998, the editors of five independent newspapers were charged with disseminating misinformation because of their Kosovo coverage. The Belgrade city prosecutor, Mjedrak Tmusic, accused the editors of *Danas*, *Blic*, *Dnevni Telegraf*, *Demokratiya*, and *Naša Borba* "because they published articles, editorials and headlines and broadcast programs which encouraged actions of terrorist gangs in Kosovo and misrepresented measures taken by the Serbian

---

[109]ANEM Alert, July 3, 1998.

Interior Ministry against terrorists in Kosovo-Metohija."[110] The charges were later dropped.

Independent radio and television stations face even more restraints, including the confiscation of radio equipment and arbitrary bans. The least obvious but most effective restriction is the deliberate lack of a coherent legal framework for the establishment of private radio and television stations, which the government uses to justify the denial of broadcast licenses.[111]

The complex and contradictory set of media laws at the Serbian republic and the federal level has made it exceedingly difficult, if not impossible, for independent radio or television stations to obtain a frequency license. At the same time, stations that were either blatantly pro-Milošević or, at least, strictly commercial and wholly uncritical, have regularly obtained licenses for broadcasts

---

[110]"Prosecutor Takes Action Against Media Over Coverage of Clashes," Tanjug, March 6, 1998.

[111]The broadcast media in Serbia is regulated by the following laws:
A) Federal laws
  1. Law on Telecommunications of the Socialist Federal Republic of Yugoslavia (SFRY)
  2. Law on Mass Media of SFRY
B) Laws of the Republic of Serbia
  1. Law on the System of Communication
  2. Law on Mass Media
  3. Law on Radio and Television
A number of other state bodies are involved in media regulation, including the Ministry of Transport and Telecommunications, the Ministry of Information, and the commercial courts. Relevant laws include the Law on Companies, the Law on Procedure for Entry into the Court Register, the Law on Unified Classification of Operation and Units of Classification, as well as a series of regulations for the implementation of these laws.

When viewed together, these law and regulations create an unnavigable maze of legal obstructions for private media outlets. For example, under current regulations, the Yugoslav Ministry of Transport and Telecommunications requires applicants for a broadcast license to prove that the station has been registered as a media company at the Ministry of Information and at the appropriate commercial court. But these documents cannot be obtained without first having a license from the Ministry of Transport and Telecommunications.

Even taken individually, Serbia and Yugoslavia's media law and regulations do not guarantee that broadcast licenses will be allocated on a non-discriminatory basis. Article 5 of Serbia's Law on Radio and Television, for example, gives the government a very broad right to grant licenses, while Article 10 (6) of the same law allows the government to revoke licenses under vague terms.

in large parts of the country. Despite numerous promises, the government has failed to introduce legislation that would allow private stations to obtain broadcast licenses, satellite link-ups, or Internet connections in a fair and apolitical manner.

An estimated 400 private radio and television stations have generally been allowed to broadcast, but they are prone to summary closure by the government, as happened to seventy-seven stations in mid-1997, and to four stations in 1998. Most often the state justifies such a closure by claiming that the station in question did not have the proper license to broadcast. This is usually true, but the lack of a license is due to the government's persistent refusal to grant licenses to any station that broadcasts independent or critical news.

On February 7, 1998, the government unexpectedly announced that a public tender would be held for radio and television stations to obtain temporary broadcast licenses. According to the government, it was intended to "create order in the airwaves" since "pirate" stations had proliferated. But the questionable legality of the tender, and the secretive and misleading manner in which it was administered, suggested that the government was devising another legal ruse to hinder the free press. The results of the tender, announced on May 16, 1998, proved these fears to be true: the vast majority of independent radio and television stations that applied were denied licenses, while numerous stations with close business or political ties to the ruling elite were granted permission to broadcast, including a radio station owned by Milošević's son, Marko, and a television station connected with his daughter, Marija.

For the stations that did get licenses, the government imposed exorbitantly high licensing fees, as much as U.S.$40,000 per month for a television station in Belgrade. The fees were later reduced, but they are still prohibitively high for most stations, especially in Montenegro. Six Yugoslav nongovernmental organizations have challenged the legality of the fees before the Yugoslav Constitutional Court.

The second stage of the tender process is officially still open, since stations were granted an opportunity to resubmit their applications. But the behavior of the government again suggests that most independent stations will be denied licenses. Some stations were not informed of the results from the first round. Other stations that did not get a frequency because of "missing documents" have been denied those documents (such as building permits) by their local authorities.

The frequency tender and the court cases against newspaper editors are consistent with the Yugoslav government's media policy over the past decade. Milošević regularly applies pressure on the independent media in times of conflict, as there is now with Kosovo.

The attacks on the media intensified as NATO threatened airstrikes in October. Serbian Deputy Prime Minister Vojislav Šešelj, head of the Serbian Radical Party, made some direct threats to the independent media, especially those Serbs working for the foreign media. In a press conference in Belgrade on October 1, he proclaimed:

> To those who we prove have participated in the service of foreign propaganda -- and those are the Voice of America, Deutsche Welle, Radio Free Europe, Radio France International, and the BBC radio service etc. -- if we find them in the moment of aggression they shouldn't expect anything good.[112]

On October 8, the Serbian government passed a Decree on Special Measures that allowed for the direct censorship of local and foreign media. The decree banned the broadcast of foreign news programs like the BBC, RFE, and VOA, and ordered local media not to disseminate material that was "against the territorial integrity, sovereignty and independence of the country." On the basis of the decree, the police closed down two newspapers, *Danas* and *Dnevni Telegraf*, and confiscated their computers on October 13. The next day, the independent daily *Naša Borba* was also closed. Two radio stations, Radio Index and Radio Senta, were also shut down.

On October 20, the Serbian parliament adopted a new Law on Public Information that incorporated many of the restrictions from the special decree, notably a ban on foreign radio and television broadcasts that were "of a political-propaganda nature." The law imposed exorbitantly high fines, as much as $100,000, on those who breach the law. On October 23, the owner of *Dnevni Telegraf* and *Evropljanin* magazine, Slavko Curuvija, was charged with publicizing information "jeopardizing the territorial integrity and independence of the Republic of Serbia and Federal Republic of Yugoslavia" because of an open letter to Milošević published in his magazine on October 19 that strongly criticized the government.[113] On October 24, Curuvija, the editor-in-chief, Dragan Bujošević and the publishing editor, Ivan Tadić, were found guilty and fined a total of $230,000.

---

[112]*Danas*, October 2, 1998.

[113]The open letter, entitled "What Next, Milošević?", blamed the government for leading Serbia into "lawlessness, fear, terror and dictatorship."

Restrictions on the Foreign Media

The first problem faced by foreign journalists covering Kosovo is in obtaining a visa for the Federal Republic of Yugoslavia. Many journalists have either had to wait long periods to get a visa, or have been denied outright, especially if they have a reputation for critical reporting and are, therefore, considered "anti-Serb" in the eyes of the government.[114] Some foreign journalists have also been attacked in the state-run media, accused of "biased" and "anti-Serb" reporting.[115]

The government has repeatedly complained about the foreign media's "one-sided" reporting in the Kosovo crisis. In a letter sent to the international press on August 31, Serbian Secretary of Information Alexander Vucic said:

> After a deluge of sensational and false reports blaming only one side for everything that happened in the former Yugoslavia—the Serbian people—many reporters and media are directly accountable for the political moves of their governments, and indirectly for the death, persecution and living-on-the-verge-of-death of the Serbs.[116]

On August 12, the Yugoslav government declared a journalist with the German newspaper *Die Tageszeitung* persona non grata because he "created and spread evil lies." Erich Rathfelder, who had been covering Kosovo since 1987, had reported witness statements about mass graves of Albanians killed by the police in Orahovac, which have not been confirmed.[117] Rathfelder also claims he was

---

[114]According to Freimut Duve, the Media Representative of the OSCE, Milada Jedrysik and Jerzy Gumowski from the Polish newspaper *Gazeta Wyborcza*, an Austrian cameraman Friedrich Wedan and a German television reporter, Hasim Hosny, have been denied visas. "Duve Kritisiert Serbiens Regierung," *Die Tageszeitung*, August 28, 1998.

[115]See *Politika*, August 4, 1998, for an article attacking the journalist Halim Hosny, with the German television station ZDF, and Roy Gutman, a reporter for the American newspaper *Newsday*.

[116]"Serb Information minister complains of biased reports," Reuters, August 31, 1998.

[117]"Taz-Korrespondent Erhält Einreiseverbot in Jugoslavien," *Die Tageszeitung*, August 13, 1998.

threatened by the police during his last trip to Kosovo on August 2. In an opinion piece published in his newspaper, he said:

> I was stopped by five policemen who, after the remark, "You were in Drenica after all," pointed their weapons at me. They threatened to confiscate my car and to arrest me. The intervention of a Dutch journalist who was following behind me in his car resulted in a calming of tempers.[118]

On August 14, Friedhelm Brebeck and his two cameramen with the German television station ARD were expelled from the Federal Republic of Yugoslavia and barred from entry into the country for three years. The government accused Brebeck of inciting Albanians to set a house in Junik on fire—an accusation Brebeck has categorically denied.[119] According to Brebeck, the Yugoslav Army checked his footage of Junik and returned it, leading him to believe it was acceptable. On the morning of August 14, however, the police arrived at the Grand Hotel in Priština, demanded the passports of Brebeck and his two colleagues, and told them that they would be escorted to the border with Macedonia.[120]

Foreign journalists also report increased difficulty in obtaining accreditation from the Secretary of Information in Priština, which is necessary to get through checkpoints throughout Kosovo. In August, the Secretary of Information's office reduced its working hours to two hours a day, and stopped putting translators' names on the accreditation document, which made it more difficult for them to get through police checkpoints.

Some foreign journalists have been physically assaulted or shot at by the police. On June 22, 1998, two journalists from the Danish television TV2, Neils Brinch and Heinrik Gram, and their Albanian interpreter were fired upon while in their armored car by the Serbian police near Glogovac.[121] No one was injured.

---

[118]"Man Wollte Mich Loswerden," *Die Tageszeitung*, August 17, 1998.

[119]IFEX Action Alert, August 18, 1998.

[120]"Serben Erobern Verlassene Stadt im Kosovo," *Die Tageszeitung*, August 17, 1998, and "Jugoslavien Weist ARD-Journalisten Aus," *Die Tageszeitung*, August 15, 1998.

[121]IFEX Action Alert, June 23, 1998.

On March 6, a BBC cameraman and an Albanian translator were secretly filming the demolition of houses in Prekaz by the police, one day after the large-scale police attack on the village (see section on Abuses in Drenica). The police fired at them with automatic weapons from a distance as they tried to leave. Both men lay down for about five minutes, but were shot at again when they got up to run away. A bullet hit the journalist's cell phone which was hanging on his waist, causing a large bruise. The Albanian translator, who wished to remain anonymous, was hit in the shoulder, but the bullet did not penetrate his bullet proof vest. After some time, they managed to get away safely.[122]

Taras Protsyuk, a Ukrainian cameraman working for Reuters TV, was knocked to the ground from behind by plainclothes policemen as he filmed a street protest in Priština on March 19, 1998. On the same day, a Belgian cameraman working for RTBF in Belgium, Michel Rousez, was beaten by the police near the university.[123]

On July 6, 1998, two correspondents traveling with a convoy of foreign diplomats were assaulted by men believed to be plainclothes policemen. Kurt Schork of Reuters reportedly shouted at the driver of a car he thought had been driving recklessly. The driver hit Schork in the face, sending his glasses flying. Anthony Lloyd from the *Times* of London came to his assistance and was kicked in the ribs.[124]

---

[122]Human Rights Watch interview, Priština, May 22, 1998.

[123]Letter to President Slobodan Milošević from the Committee to Protect Journalists, March 20, 1998.

[124]Committee to Protect Journalists, "British Correspondents Roughed Up in Kosovo," New York, July 8, 1998.

10. VIOLATIONS OF THE RULES OF WAR BY THE UÇK

The rules of internal armed conflict, outlined in Common Article 3 and Protocol II of the Geneva Conventions, are binding on both governments and armed insurgencies. As such, the UÇK is legally obliged to respect the provisions of international humanitarian law, such as the protection of noncombatants and the prohibition of hostage taking. (See section on Legal Standards and the Kosovo Conflict.)

Despite these obligations, the UÇK has committed violations of international humanitarian law, including the taking of hostages and, by their own apparent admission, summary executions (see below). At least 138 individuals, mostly ethnic Serbs (but also some ethnic Albanians and Roma) are feared abducted by the UÇK.

Some UÇK operations were apparently intended to drive ethnic Serbs out of their villages. Human Rights Watch heard credible reports of ethnic Serbs being forced to leave the villages of Jelovac, Kijevo, Leočina, Gorni Ratiš, Maznik, Dašinovac, Veliki Djurdjevak, Mlečane, Dubrava, Boksić, and Lugodjija. In a number of cases, elderly Serbs refused to leave, either too old to flee or unwilling to abandon their homes. Some of these people are currently missing and feared dead (see below).

The UÇK has attacked and seized some ethnic Albanians and Roma who it considers "collaborators" with the Yugoslav government. According to the Serbian Ministry of Internal Affairs, from January to May 1998, the UÇK attacked twenty-eight ethnic Albanians, killing four and injuring five.[125] Although it is still unconfirmed, some diplomats, humanitarian aid workers and journalists in Kosovo believe that the UÇK planted the landmines south of Likovac, which used to be a UÇK base (see chapter on the Use of Landmines).

Spokesmen for the UÇK have repeatedly stressed the UÇK's willingness to respect the rules of war, although their statements raise doubts about their interpretation of these norms. The prohibition on summary executions appears to be misunderstood, particularly in the case of ethnic Albanians suspected of collaboration with government forces, and Serbian civilians considered a part of the local security apparatus.

In an interview given to the Albanian-language newspaper *Koha Ditore* on July 11, 1998, UÇK spokesman Jakup Krasniqi said:

---

[125]"Terrorism in Kosmet in Numbers and Pictures," taken from the website of the Serbian Secretary of Information (www.serbia-info.com).

[T]he UÇK has never dealt with civilians, or only if they have been in the service of the army and the police and have done serious harm to the people and the Albanian national cause. There have been cases in which they have been kidnaped, but in this event they have been handed over to international organizations, of course when they have been innocent.

First of all, all Serbian forces, whether the police, the military, or armed civilians, are our enemy. From the start, we had our own internal rules for our operations. These clearly lay down that the UÇK recognizes the Geneva Conventions and the conventions governing the conduct of war, even though it has not been offered the chance of signing them, as it would have done. We do not go in for kidnaping. Even if some people have suffered, these have been more Albanian collaborators than Serbian civilians. We do not deal with civilians, and we return those whom we take as prisoners of war. A few days ago we handed over two Serbs originating from Croatia to the International Red Cross. Those we have kidnaped are either announced in a list or reported to be executed, but we do not behave in a base fashion like Serbia.[126]

Shaban Shala, a UÇK commander who used to be an activist with the Council for the Defense of Human Rights and Freedoms in Glogovac, said that the UÇK General Headquarters would not order human rights abuses, but that some fighters may "make mistakes":

I say this with complete responsibility—the UÇK is called as such because it really is a liberation army. It is not engaged in conflict to harm others. It never made any attempts to usurp property, to destroy property that belongs to others; it did not abduct or massacre innocent children, women, or elderly. We are at war with the Serbian police and military forces, as well as other Serb paramilitary formations. We are not at war with civilians, innocent people, with children and the handicapped.

[126]"Spokesman Explains Structure of Rebel Army," BBC Summary of World Broadcasts, from Koha Ditore in Albanian, July 12, 1998, and "Koha Ditore Interview with Jakup Krasniqi, UÇK Spokesman - Part II," Arta, July 12, 1998.

I can add in this context that the UÇK General Headquarters has not and will not issue an order to pursue, kill, or massacre innocent people, or loot or destroy Serbian property. However, not everything can be controlled during a war. There are cases when individuals make mistakes, but such cases are punished by the UÇK, even if its soldiers conducted them.[127]

More recently, the UÇK's newly-appointed political representative, Adem Demaçi, told Radio B92 from Belgrade:

When I talked to certain people from the headquarters, I saw that there was a united view on one thing: we do not deal in kidnapings. If some groups do it on their own, and if we have influence on them, we always intervene and kidnaped persons are released.[128]

On September 9, the police announced that they had found the bodies of people they claimed had been killed by the UÇK near Glodjane in a canal near Lake Radonjić. By September 16, they had gathered thirty-four bodies, eleven of whom were identified, including some ethnic Albanians. As of September 23, the identification process was ongoing.[129]

The most serious allegation made against the UÇK prior to the September 9 announcement was the Yugoslav government's accusation that in the village of Klečka the UÇK had executed twenty-two civilians, including women and children, and burned the bodies. The police claimed to have discovered human remains and a kiln used to cremate the bodies when they recaptured Klečka from the UÇK on August 27. The details of the execution-style killings were provided by two ethnic Albanians who the Yugoslav authorities said were UÇK fighters. One of them, Bekim Mazreku, was presented to foreign reporters while in police custody and then questioned by Danica Marinković, an investigating judge from Priština who has been involved in a number of political trials in which ethnic Albanians were

---

[127]"Koha Ditore Interview with UÇK Commander," Arta, July 25, 1998.

[128]"Demaçi Will Contact Main Headquarters of UÇK," Radio B92, August 26, 1998.

[129]Among those identified were: Ilire Frakaj, Jusuf Hoxha, Milos Radunović and Slobodan Radosević.

tortured.[130] Mazreku was not allowed to speak independently to the journalists.[131] According to the *New York Times*, "one man, whose videotaped interrogation was made available to the *New York Times* today, gave accounts that did not make sense and which the police say they cannot corroborate."[132]

UÇK spokesmen rejected the charges, saying that the UÇK, "has not killed a single Serb civilian."[133] The two ethnic Albanians presented by the police and interviewed by Danica Marinković were not members of the UÇK, they claimed.

As of September 1, 1998, Human Rights Watch was not able to confirm the charges about Klečka. The manner in which the allegations were made raise serious questions about their validity and underline the importance of an investigation by an impartial forensics team.

Abductions of Ethnic Serbs

The precise number of people held by the UÇK is difficult to determine since the UÇK does not provide public information on those in its custody, and a number of people have been held hostage and then released. Estimates of human rights and humanitarian organizations working on the ground range from one hundred to 140. According to the International Committee for the Red Cross, as of September, 138 ethnic Serbs were believed to have been taken by the UÇK.

The Humanitarian Law Center, which has been monitoring detentions and abductions by the police and the UÇK, has documented 103 ethnic Serbs who were unaccounted for as of August 1998, thirty-nine of whom were last seen in UÇK custody. The center also documented the cases of three ethnic Albanians abducted

---

[130]See, for example, the case of Destan Rukiqi in the section on Detentions and Arrests and "Persecution Persist: Human Rights Violations in Kosovo," Human Rights Watch/Helsinki report, December 1996.

[131]*Reuters*, August 29, 1998.

[132]Micheal O'Connor, "Rebel Terror Forcing Minority Serbs Out of Kosovo, The *New York Times*, August 30, 1998.

[133]Agence France Press, August 30, 1998.

by the UÇK, ostensibly because they were considered "collaborators" with the Yugoslav government, whose whereabouts are currently unknown.[134]

According to a statement from the Yugoslav Ministry of Foreign Affairs issued on August 31, 1998, Albanian "terrorists" had abducted 178 individuals in Kosovo, including 128 ethnic Serbs and Montenegrins, forty-two ethnic Albanians, and six ethnic Roma. Out of this group, thirty-nine were released, seven escaped, and sixteen had been killed, leaving 114 people still in UÇK detention.[135]

According to the Serbian Ministry of Internal Affairs, 233 civilians were "kidnapped" from January 1 to September 13 (157 Serbs and Montenegrins, 67 Albanians, 6 Roma, 1 Macedonian, 1 Muslim, and 1 Bulgarian), as well as ten policemen.[136]

Below are some specific cases:

Abductions in Orahovac

On July 19, the UÇK began its first major attack on a larger city: Orahovac. An estimated eighty-five ethnic Serbs were taken into custody by the UÇK, although thirty-five of them were subsequently released. As of August 1998, at least forty people were still unaccounted for.

During the attack, approximately thirty elderly Serbs took shelter in the Monastery of Saints Cosmas and Damian in Zočiste village together with seven monks and one nun. According to the Serbian Orthodox Church, the monastery was attacked for forty-five minutes with light artillery and machine guns and the guest house was damaged by two grenades.[137] Local Serbs told the Humanitarian Law Center, however, that the monks had resisted for two hours with four rifles before they realized a defense was futile and surrendered.[138] Everyone inside the monastery was taken to a school in nearby Semetište.

---

[134]Humanitarian Law Center, "Kosovo - Disappearances in Times of Armed Conflict," Spotlight Report No. 27, August 5, 1998.

[135]Statement Yugoslav Ministry of Foreign Affairs, Belgrade, August 31, 1998.

[136]"Who is Violating Human Rights in Kosovo and Metohija," Republic of Serbia, Ministry of Internal Affairs, September 1998.

[137]Press Release of the Serbian Orthodox Diocese of Raska and Prizren, July 22, 1998.

[138]Humanitarian Law Center, "Kosovo - Disappearances in Times of Armed Conflict," Spotlight Report No. 27, August 5, 1998.

According to the ICRC and numerous media sources, the UÇK handed thirty-five of these people over to the ICRC unharmed on July 22, including the seven Orthodox monks, one nun and twenty-five elderly people.[139] According to the Humanitarian Law Center, another ten people detained in the Orahovac offensive were released on the night of July 29-30, including Slavka, Snežana, and Ninoslav Baljošević.[140]

The fate of an estimated forty other people taken from the Orahovac area, however, remains unknown. They include: Tomislav Baljošević and his son Saša, Duško Dolasević, Srdjan and Srecko Vitosević, Djordje Djorić, Duško Djonović, Sinisa Lukić, Veselin Lazić, Dusko Patranogić, Predrag Djurdjić, Jovan Vasić and Rajko Nikolić, plus five members of the Bozanić family: Mladen, Nemanja, Tihomir, Novica and Boško, and eight members of the Kostić family: Lazar, Todor, Saska, Miroljub, Vekoslav, Srecko, Svetomir, and Vitko. There are also reports of seventeen other people abducted by the UÇK from the village of Retimlje near Orahovac.

Jovan Lukić

According to Tanjug and the Humanitarian Law Center, Jovan Lukić was detained by a group of armed Albanians while driving near Orahovac. Tanjug reported that Lukić was detained on July 19 along with Veselin Lazić, but the center mentions only Lukić being detained on July 17.[141]

Lukić told the center that he was held in Mališevo with a group of prisoners, including Srdjan and Srecko Vitošević, a Roma man named Azem with his wife and daughter, a man named Duško from Orahovac, a man named Toma and his son, two doctors from Orahovac, and a doctor from Velika Hoča. The male detainees, he said, were taken out in small groups by a van that returned empty. Lukić was eventually taken in the van with some others, their hands tied, to a place in the woods. He succeeded in freeing his hands, however, and after struggling with one of the armed Albanians, managed to escape. He told the center that he does not know what happened to the other prisoners.

---

[139]"Federal Republic of Yugoslavia/Kosovo: ICRC Aid for Conflict Victims," ICRC News 98/30, July 29, 1998, and "Kidnaped Serbs Released," AFP, July 22, 1998.

[140]Humanitarian Law Center, "Kosovo - Disappearances in Times of Armed Conflict."

[141]"Terrorist Abduct Two Serbs," Tanjug, July 20, 1998, and Humanitarian Law Center, "Kosovo - Disappearances in Times of Armed Conflict."

Ratko and Branko Staletić

The police found the bodies of Ratko Staletić and his son Branko on July 30 near Orlate village on the Priština-Peć road, according to the Humanitarian Law Center. The two residents of Mlečane village had reportedly been taken by ethnic Albanians in military uniforms on June 20, 1998.[142]

Vojko and Ivan Bakrać

Vojko and Ivan Bakrać, two ethnic Serb refugees from Croatia, and two other ethnic Serbs were taken off a bus on the Prizren-Štimlje road by armed ethnic Albanians on June 29. Vojko and Ivan Bakrać were on their way to the UNHCR offices in Priština, because they had been accepted in a United States resettlement program for ethnic Serb refugees in Kosovo.[143] According to the Humanitarian Law Center, they were released on July 8 or 9, although the two other Serbs, whose identities are unknown, remain unaccounted for.[144]

Ten Employees of the Belaćevac Mine

On June 22, the UÇK took control of the Belaćevac mine, a large coal mine near the town of Obilić. The police recaptured the mine a few days later. The UÇK reportedly captured nine ethnic Serbs in Obilić on July 22 as they were on their way to work at the mine; they were Dušan Andjančić, Pero Andjančić, Zoran Andjančić, Mirko Buha, Filip Gojković, Božidar Lempić, Srboljub Savić, Mirko Trifunović and Dragan Vukmirović. None of them has been heard from since. The *Times* of London cites a senior Serbian policeman as saying that negotiations between the police and the UÇK over the nine workers had "broken down" before the police retook control of the mine. A local miner, Nebojsa Janković was reportedly told that his nine colleagues had been "executed," but this could not be confirmed.[145]

---

[142]Humanitarian Law Center, "Kosovo - Disappearances in Times of Armed Conflict."

[143]Human Rights Watch interview with UNHCR, Brussels, June 15, 1998.

[144]Humanitarian Law Center, "Kosovo - Disappearances in Times of Armed Conflict."

[145]Tom Walker, "Guerrillas in Kosovo 'Killed Mine Hostages'," *Times* (London), July 2, 1998.

Oliver Zalić

On June 22, the *New York Times* reported the death of Oliver Zalić, an ethnic Serb from Bica village who, according to his family, was killed by ethnic Albanians in front of his house while defending his sister and mother.[146]

Milosav, Sultana, Radomir, Aleksandra, and Dostana Šmigić

By May 1998, most ethnic Serbs in Leočina had left their homes after threats from local Albanians. Five members of the Šmigić family, however, four of them over seventy years old, decided not to leave their village. One of them, Krstiva Šmigić, told the Humanitarian Law Center that ethnic Albanians in military uniforms entered their yard around 10 a.m. on July 9. She managed to escape but Milosav (75), Sultana (72), Radomir (54), Aleksandra (c. 75), and Dostana (42) have not been heard from since:

> Us three women [Sultana, Aleksandra and Dostana] left the house and went into the fields. After a while, Sultana and Lenka said they wanted to go back. Sultana went to her husband, and me and Lenka went back to her house, to Radomir. But about thirty of them [ethnic Albanians] were going into the yard and, when they saw us, they came toward us. They were armed, some in uniform and some in civilian clothes. Ten of them went into Radomir's house. They found him upstairs. We heard screams and Lenka rushed upstairs. I stayed below. I heard terrible screams and moaning from above. I couldn't bear it any more and went out again. I heard three rifle shots before I got into some high grass.[147]

Krstiva said she saw Milosav's house in flames from her hiding spot. After two days, she made it to the town of Rudnik, where she reported the incident to the police. On May 19, Krstiva Šmigić's daughter, Dostana, went back to Leočina to

---

[146]Michael O'Connor, "Kosovo Rebels' New Tactic: Attack Serb Civilians," the *New York Times*, June 24, 1998.

[147]Humanitarian Law Center, "Kosovo - Disappearances in Times of Armed Conflict."

get her mother and three relatives. She was then abducted, reportedly in Ozrim, and has not been heard from since.[148]

Zivorad Spasić

Zivorad Spasić, a driver for the Mitrovica power plant, was last seen on May 10, 1998. His father, from a village near Obilić, asked the Council for the Defense of Human Rights and Freedoms and the Democratic League of Kosovo for help in finding his son.

Slobodan, Milica and Miloš Radošević

Slobodan (64), Milica (59), and Miloš (60) Radošević were the only ethnic Serbs to stay behind in Dašinovac village when the UÇK took control on April 22. On September 16, the police announced that the bodies of Miloš and Slobodan Radošević had been found in a canal that feeds into Lake Radonic near Glodjane.

According to the Humanitarian Law Center and Amnesty International, Rosa Radošević tried to go back to Dašinovac the next day with her son Staniša to look for her husband Slobodan. They were stopped in Požar village at a UÇK checkpoint and taken to UÇK headquarters in Glodjane, where Staniša was reportedly beaten.[149]

Dara and Vukosava Vujošević, Milka, and Milovan Vlahović

According to both the Humanitarian Law Center and Amnesty International, most ethnic Serbs fled their homes in Gornji Ratiš on April 21 when the UÇK took control of the village. Dara (69) and Vukosava (65) Vujošević and Milka (62) and Milovan (60) Vlahović decided to stay and their whereabouts are currently unknown.[150]

---

[148]See Michael O'Connor, "Rebel Terror Forcing Minority Serbs Out of Kosovo," the *New York Times*, August 30, 1998, and *Blic* newspaper, May 21, 1998.

[149]Amnesty International, "Human Rights Violations Against Women in Kosovo Province," and Humanitarian Law Center, "Kosovo - Disappearances in Times of Armed Conflict."

[150]"Human Rights Violations Against Women in Kosovo Province," A Human Rights Crisis in Kosovo Province, Document Series B #1, Amnesty International, August 1998, and Humanitarian Law Center, "Kosovo - Disappearances in Times of Armed Conflict."

Abductions of Roma

According to the Humanitarian Law Center and the newspaper *Blic*, Gurim Bejta and Agron Beriša, both Roma, and Ivan Zarić, an ethnic Serb, left Dolac on May 20 for the village of Grabanica. As of August 1998, their whereabouts were still unknown.[151]

Human Rights Watch heard unconfirmed reports that four armed ethnic Albanians dragged Ramadan Uka and his wife, both Roma, from their homes in Budisavci near Peć at the end of March 1998. According to a center researcher who spoke with Mr. Uka, the Albanians, whom Ramadan knew, beat him and raped his wife, but his story could not be confirmed.[152]

Abductions of Ethnic Albanians

Since the intensification of it activities in 1996, the UÇK has targeted ethnic Albanians it considers "collaborators" with the Yugoslav government.

According to the Serbian Orthodox Monastery at Visoki Dečani near Dečan,two elderly ethnic Albanians, Hajdar Kuci and Beki Cacaj, were killed near the Bistrica river outside of Dečan on May 7. The next day, unknown armed individuals attacked a van from the nearby power plant. An ethnic Albanian, Vehbi Mustafa (65), was killed, while four ethnic Serbs, Boško Vlahovič, Esad Muminovič, Miso Mijovič, and Dragan Djurisič were injured.[153]

According to the pro-government Priština Media Center, the UÇK abducted three ethnic Albanians from Donji Godanc on June 26: Agim Ademi, Veseli Ahmeti and Shucrija Zymeri.

As of September 16, forensics experts were still conducting investigations on the thirty-two bodies found near Lake Radonjić. Two ethnic Albanians had been identified: Ilire Frakaj and Jusuf Hoxha.

---

[151]*Blic* newspaper, May 21, 1991, and Humanitarian Law Center, "Kosovo - Disappearances in Times of Armed Conflict."

[152]Human Rights Watch interview with Humanitarian Law Center researcher, Priština, May 21, 1998.

[153]Press Release of the Brotherhood of the Serbian Orthodox Monastery at Visoki Dečani, May 9, 1998, Dečan. The Council for the Defense of Human Rights and Freedoms also reported on Mustafa's death, but implied that he had been shot by police or the military. "Another Albanian Killed in Deçan," Press Release of the Council for the Defense of Human Rights and Freedoms, May 8, 1998.

Restrictions on the Media

The UÇK has periodically restricted the domestic and international media in Kosovo by denying access to certain areas, detaining and, on a few occasions, physically attacking journalists. On August 21, 1998, an ethnic Serbian journalist with the state-run Radio Priština, Djuro Slavuj, and his driver, Ranko Perinić, went missing near the city of Orahovac, and were feared abducted by the UÇK. According to the Radio Priština office, the two left Orahovac for the nearby town of Malisevo in a blue Zastava car, but never arrived.[154] As of October 25, 1998, their whereabouts were still unknown.

On August 26, the UÇK's newly appointed political representative, Adem Demaçi, said that he would try to secure the journalists' release, although he didn't know if the group that abducted the journalists was under the control of "UÇK headquarters."[155] Six days later, UÇK spokesman Jakup Krasniqi said the UÇK knows nothing about the journalists' abduction. In an interview with the Albanian-language *Koha Ditore*, he said:

> We know nothing about the arrest or the kidnaping of any Serb resident or journalist. The UÇK did not pick up weapons to fight Serb residents or journalists, but to fight against Serb terrorists and soldiers, that turned Kosova into a burnt land. After all this terror and destruction seen in Kosova, it is impossible to control the feelings of hate and revenge that have been planted by the enemy itself, despite our insistence that the Albanian war does not take the features of the barbarous war conducted by the enemy.[156]

On October 18, two more Serbian journalists were captured, reportedly by the UÇK. Nebojša Radošević, a journalist for Tanjug, the state-run news agency, and a Tanjug photographer, Vladimir Dobrićić, went missing near the village of Magura. By October 23, the International Committee of the Red Cross (ICRC) had confirmed that the two men were being held by the UÇK. According to the ICRC,

---

[154]Human Rights Watch telephone interview with editor at Radio Priština, August 26, 1998.

[155]"Demaçi Will Contact Main Headquarters of UCK," Radio B92, August 26, 1998.

[156]*Koha Ditore*, September 1, 1998.

the UÇK said that the two journalists were in good health but that they were under "investigation" for spying. If innocent, the UÇK told the ICRC, they will be released.[157]

In July, three Russian journalists were reportedly detained by members of the UÇK. According to Reporters Sans Frontieres, on July 18, Sergei Mitim from the newspaper *Izvestia* was detained and reportedly beaten by members of a UÇK patrol on the Glogovac-Srbica road. He was released after several hours, but his film and rented car were taken.[158] On July 20, Oleg Safiulin and Oleg Galanov, with the TV program Vesti, were reportedly interrogated for several hours by the UÇK and then released.[159]

On August 14, freelance journalist Stacy Sullivan was in Glodjane interviewing ethnic Albanian civilians with two UÇK escorts present. According to Sullivan, another UÇK member drove up and demanded she stop. He grabbed her notebook and burned some pages that contained interviews of ethnic Albanian refugees she had taken over the past three days. Later, this UÇK member and her two escorts drove to the regional command headquarters near Vranoc. The commander in charge apologized to Sullivan for the soldier's actions and said that he had stripped the soldier of his weapons, although whether this happened could not be confirmed.[160]

Restrictions on Humanitarian Aid Workers

On July 23, 1998, UÇK fighters at a checkpoint in Lodja near Peć confiscated a vehicle belonging to Medecins Sans Frontieres, but the vehicle was returned some days later.[161]

In early September 1998, a UÇK checkpoint turned back a UNHCR convoy for the first time. According to UNHCR, a convoy with five tons of ready-to-eat meals was blocked while heading to the village of Golubovac.

---

[157]Human Rights Watch telephone interview with ICRC, October 22, 1998.

[158]IFEX Action Alert, July 21, 1998.

[159]"Two Russian Journalists Taken Hostage by Albanian Militants," Itar-Tass, July 21, 1998.

[160]Human Rights Watch interview with Stacy Sullivan, New York, September 3, 1998.

[161]"Kosovo Rebels Confiscate an MSF Vehicle," Agence France Presse, July 24, 1998.

UNHCR spokesman Kris Janowski said that UÇK soldiers blocked the convoy because of shelling, which could be heard a short distance away. But the rebels also suggested that the UNHCR convoy leader and driver were spies.[162]

According to diplomatic sources, the UÇK turned back a truck at an undisclosed location with five tons of food from the World Food Program on September 7, 1998, because the driver of the truck was an ethnic Serb.

---

[162]Wendy Lubetkin, "UN Appeals for Funds to Avert Catastrophe in Kosovo this Winter," September 8, 1998, USIA European Correspondent.

11. LEGAL STANDARDS AND THE KOSOVO CONFLICT

International Law

Until 1998, human rights abuses in Kosovo, as documented in numerous human rights reports,[163] were evaluated against the norms of international human rights law. Police abuse, arbitrary arrests, and violations of due process constituted violations of, among other instruments, the Universal Declaration of Human Rights and the International Covenant on Civil and Political Rights, which the Yugoslav government has pledged to respect.[164]

The growth of armed opposition by the UÇK, however, and the intensification of fighting between government forces and this armed insurgency, have altered the nature of the conflict in Kosovo. Since February, intense fighting has resulted in an estimated six hundred deaths and the displacement of 300,000 persons, while hundreds of villages have been destroyed. Documented abuses include extrajudicial executions, the use of disproportionate force, indiscriminate attacks against civilians, and the systematic destruction of civilian property by the Serbian special police and Yugoslav Army, as well as abuses, such as hostage taking and summary executions, committed against Serbian and Albanian civilians by the UÇK.

By all estimations, the Yugoslav government is fighting against an armed insurgency that has waged ongoing and concerted attacks against the Serbian police and Yugoslav Army, and has controlled large sections of Kosovo, albeit temporarily. In terms of international law, the confrontation is considered an "armed conflict."

The conduct of both government forces and the armed insurgency in an armed conflict is governed by international humanitarian law, known as the rules of war, and in particular Article 3 common to the four 1949 Geneva Conventions, Protocol II to those conventions, and the customary laws of war.[165] Like human

---

[163]Human Rights Watch reports include: *Increasing Turbulence: Human Rights in Yugoslavia*, October 1989; *Yugoslavia: Crisis in Kosovo*, with the International Helsinki Federation, March 1990; *Yugoslavia: Human Rights Abuses in Kosovo 1990-1992*, October 1992; *Open Wounds: Human Rights Abuses in Kosovo*, March 1993; *Persecution Persists: Human Rights Violations in Kosovo*, December 1996.

[164]Yugoslavia ratified the International Covenant on Civil and Political Rights on June 2, 1971.

[165]Yugoslavia acceded to the four Geneva Conventions on April 21, 1950, and to Protocols I and II on June 11, 1979.

rights law, humanitarian law prohibits summary executions, torture, and other inhuman treatment and the application of ex post facto law. The essential difference is that the provisions of humanitarian law that apply in times of armed conflict are not derogable nor capable of suspension.

The special significance of the Kosovo situation having passed the threshold of an "armed conflict" is that it invokes the jurisdiction of the International Criminal Tribunal for the Former Yugoslavia, which is mandated to prosecute intra alia crimes against humanity and violations of the laws or customs of war in the territory of the former Yugoslavia.[166]

Kosovo as an Internal Armed Conflict

International humanitarian law makes a critical distinction between international and non-international (internal) armed conflicts, and a proper characterization of the conflict is important to determine which aspects of international humanitarian law apply. Article 2 common to the four Geneva Conventions of 1949 states that an international armed conflict must involve a declared war or any other armed conflict which may arise "between two or more of the High Contracting Parties" to the convention. The official commentary to the 1949 Geneva Conventions broadly defines "armed conflict" as any difference between two states leading to the intervention of armed forces.[167]

---

[166]On July 7, 1998, the Tribunal declared publicly that the hostilities in Kosovo had reached the level of an armed conflict, although the starting date for this designation was not stated. In a letter to members of the Contact Group dealing with the Kosovo crisis, Justice Louise Arbour declared:

> [T]he nature and scale of the fighting indicate that an "armed conflict", within the meaning of international law, exists in Kosovo. As a consequence, she intends to bring charges for crimes against humanity or war crimes, if evidence of such crimes is established.

The U.S. government has a similar position. On August 31, U.S. ambassador-at-large for war crimes issues, David Scheffer, said, "there is no question that an armed conflict exists in Kosovo. There is also no question that the War Crimes Tribunal has jurisdiction to investigate and prosecute war crimes and crimes against humanity committed in Kosovo pursuant to U.N. Security Council Resolution 827 (1993), which covers the former Yugoslavia."

[167]International Committee of the Red Cross, *Commentary*, III Geneva Convention (International Committee of the Red Cross: Geneva 1960), p. 23.

An internal armed conflict is more difficult to define, since it is sometimes debatable whether hostilities within a state have reached the level of an armed conflict, in contrast to tensions, disturbance, riots, or isolated acts of violence. The official commentary to Common Article 3 of the Geneva Conventions, which regulates internal armed conflicts, lists a series of conditions that, although not obligatory, provide some convenient guidelines. First and foremost among these is whether the party in revolt against the de jure government, in this case the UÇK, "possesses an organized military force, an authority responsible for its acts, acting within a determinate territory and having the means of respecting and ensuring respect for the Convention."[168]

Other conditions outlined in the convention's commentary deal with the government's response to the insurgency. Another indication that there is an internal armed conflict is the government's recognition that it is obliged to use its regular military forces against an insurgency.[169]

Internal armed conflicts that reach a higher level of hostilities are governed by the 1977 Protocol II to the Geneva Conventions, which is more encompassing than Common Article 3 in its protection of civilians (see below). Protocol II is invoked when armed conflicts:

> [T]ake place in the territory of a High Contracting Party between its armed forces and dissident armed forces or other organized armed groups which, under responsible command, exercise such control over a part of its territory as to enable them to carry out sustained and concerted military operations and to implement this Protocol.[170]

Finally, internal armed conflicts are also governed by customary international law, such as United Nations General Assembly 2444.[171] This resolution, adopted by unanimous vote on December 19, 1969, expressly

---

[168]International Committee of the Red Cross, *Commentary*, IV Geneva Convention (International Committee of the Red Cross: Geneva 1958), p. 35.

[169]Ibid.

[170]International Committee of the Red Cross Commentary to Protocol II, p. 90.

[171]U.N. General Assembly, *Respect for Human Rights in Armed Conflicts*, United Nations Resolution 2444, G.A. Res. 2444, 23 U.N. GAOR Supp. (No. 18) U.N. Doc. A/7433 (New York: U.N., 1968), p. 164.

recognized the customary law principle of civilian immunity and its complementary principle requiring the warring parties to distinguish civilians from combatants at all times. The preamble to this resolution states that these fundamental humanitarian law principles apply "in all armed conflicts," meaning both international and internal armed conflicts.[172] Interpreting its jurisdiction over violations of customs of war committed in the territory of the former Yugoslavia, the ICTY has held that this jurisdiction includes "violations of Common Article 3 and other customary rules on internal conflict" and "violations of agreements binding upon the parties to the conflict, considered qua treaty law, i.e. agreements which have not turned into customary international law" (e.g. Protocol II to the Geneva Convention).[173]

The Applicability of Common Article 3 and Protocol II to the Conflict in Kosovo

The hostilities between the UÇK and government forces had, by February 28, 1998, reached a level of conflict to which the obligations of Common Article 3 apply. Given the subsequent intensity of the conflict from March to September, Human Rights Watch is also evaluating the conduct of the UÇK and government forces based on the standards enshrined in Protocol II to the Geneva Convention.[174]

On February 28, Serbian special police forces launched their first large-scale, military attack on villages — Likošane and Ćirez— suspected of harboring UÇK members. Since that date, the UÇK and the government have been engaged in ongoing hostilities involving military offensives, front lines, and the use of

---

[172]U.N. General Assembly Resolution 2444 affirms:

. . . the following principles for observance by all government and other authorities responsible for action in armed conflicts:

(a)   That the right of the parties to a conflict to adopt means of injuring the enemy is not unlimited;

(b)   That it is prohibited to launch attacks against the civilian populations as such;

(c)   That distinction must be made at all times between persons taking part in the hostilities and members of the civilian population to the effect that the latter be spared as much as possible.

[173]The Prosecution v. Duško Tadić, Appeals Chamber Decision on the Defense Motion for Interlocutory Appeal on Jurisdiction, para. 89 (October 2, 1995).

[174]Human Rights Watch also takes some concepts from Protocol I, since it provides useful guidance on the rules of war.

attack helicopters and heavy artillery (mostly by the government). The UÇK possesses small arms and light artillery.

Although the UÇK is primarily a guerilla army with no ridged hierarchical structure, and there are separate internal factions, during the period covered by this report (from February to September) the UÇK was an organized military force for purposes of international humanitarian law. According to those close to the UÇK who were interviewed by Human Rights Watch, at least until the summer offensive by the Serbian special police and Yugoslav Army, the UÇK is believed to have had five or six "operative zones," each with a regional and several subregional commanders. Not all, but most of the regional commanders were represented in the High Command, the body within the UÇK that makes decisions for the whole UÇK. This structure allowed decisions to be transmitted down to the fighters.

Seasoned war correspondents, as well as Human Rights Watch researchers who encountered the UÇK, observed instances of discipline among UÇK fighters manning checkpoints and their tendency to apply similar policies and procedures (for example, with regard to granting journalists access to areas under UÇK control). Such discipline is an indication that the fighters were receiving orders regarding policy and that the fighters were answerable at least to regional commanders. There are also cases, however, when a clear lack of discipline was observed, which points to some structural weaknesses within the UÇK. Despite this, it is clear that the UÇK leadership was able to organize systematic attacks throughout large parts of Kosovo. It also coordinated logistical and financial support from the Albanian diaspora in Western Europe and the United States. Until the Yugoslav Army sealed the border with Albania, arms flowed regularly from Albania's north.

From April until mid-July, 1998, the UÇK held as much as 40 percent of the territory of Kosovo, although most of that territory was retaken by government forces by August 1998. Until then, however, the UÇK had held a number of strategic towns and villages, and manned checkpoints along some of Kosovo's important roads; today their area of control has been reduced to some parts of Drenica and a few scattered pockets in the west, especially at night.

It appears that its command structure has been damaged as a result of the offensive, although it is believed that the nucleus of the organization continues to exist. Complicating the matter is the recent rise of a separate armed Albanian organization known as FARK (Forcat Armatosur e Republikes se Kosoves -- Armed Forces of the Republic of Kosova), which has a separate base in Northern Albania and is mostly present in the Metohija (Dukagjin in Albanian) region of Kosovo. By September 1998, it was clear that this alternative group, comprised mostly of ethnic Albanians with past experience in the Yugoslav Army and police, did not agree with the UÇK's military strategy, criticizing its lack of professionalism. FARK, however, apparently did not exist as an organized force until August 1998.[175]

In interviews and public statements, UÇK spokesmen have also repeatedly expressed the organization's willingness to respect the rules of war, which is one of the factors to be considered in determining whether an internal armed conflict exists.[176] In an interview given to the Albanian-language newspaper *Koha Ditore* in July 1998, UÇK spokesman Jakup Krasniqi said:

> From the start, we had our own internal rules for our operations. These clearly lay down that the UÇK recognizes the Geneva Conventions and the conventions governing the conduct of war.[177]

UÇK Communique number 51, issued by "UÇK General Headquarters" on August 26, stated that, " The UÇK is an institutionalized and organized Army, is getting increasingly professional and ready to fight to victory."[178]

There are reported cases of UÇK soldiers being disciplined by their own commanders for having harassed or shot at foreign journalists, although it is unknown if any UÇK combatants have been punished for targeting ethnic Serb civilians, abusing those in detention, or any other violation of Common Article 3

---

[175]The ICRC *Commentary* to Article 1 of Protocol II addresses the requirements for control over territory. Paragraph 3.3. says: "In many conflicts there is considerable movement in the theater of hostilities; it often happens that territorial control changes hands rapidly. Sometimes domination of a territory will be relative, for example, when urban centres remain in government hands while rural areas escape their authority. In practical terms, if the insurgent armed groups are organized in accordance with the requirements of the Protocol, the extent of territory they can claim to control will be that which escapes the control of the government armed forces. However, there must be some degree of stability in the control of even a modest area of land for them to be capable of effectively applying the rules of the Protocol."

[176]The ICRC *Commentary* on Common Article 3, paragraph 1, states that an internal armed conflict exists when, "the insurgent civil authority agrees to be bound by the provisions of the Convention."

[177]*Koha Ditore*, July 12, 1998.

[178]UÇK Communique Nr. 51, as published in *Koha Ditore*, August 26, 1998.

or Protocol II. Over 100 people, mostly ethnic Serbs, are believed to have been detained by the UÇK.

Finally, through its words and actions, the Yugoslav government has clearly recognized the UÇK as an organized armed force. In addition to the special police forces, which operate similar to a military organization, the government has been obliged to use regular military forces, the Yugoslav Army, against the insurgents.

The major government offensive that began in July has severely affected the capacity of the UÇK, and may ultimately affect the status of the conflict under the laws of war. However, the conditions of Article 3 and Protocol II were satisfied during the period under the purview of this report (February - August, 1998). Human Rights Watch is, therefore, evaluating the conduct of both the government and the UÇK based on the principles outlined in Common Article 3 and Protocol II.

Common Article 3 and the Protection of Non-combatants

Article 3 common to the four Geneva Conventions has been called a convention within a convention. It is the only provision of the Geneva Conventions that directly applies to internal (as opposed to international) armed conflicts.

Common Article 3, Section 1, states:

In the case of armed conflict not of an international character occurring in the territory of one of the High Contracting Parties, each Party to the conflict shall be bound to apply, as a minimum, the following provisions:

1. Persons taking no active part in the hostilities, including members of armed forces who had laid down their arms and those placed *hors de combat* by sickness, wounds, detention, or any other cause, shall in all circumstances be treated humanely, without any adverse distinction founded on race, colour, religion or faith, sex, birth or wealth, or any other similar criteria.

    To this end the following acts are and shall remain prohibited at any time and in any place whatsoever with respect to the above-mentioned persons:

a. violence to life and person, in particular murder of all kinds, mutilation, cruel treatment and torture;

b.   taking of hostages;

c.   outrages upon personal dignity, in particular humiliating and degrading treatment;

d.   the passing of sentences and the carrying out of executions without previous judgment pronounced by a regularly constituted court, affording all the judicial guarantees which are recognized as indispensable by civilized peoples.

Common Article 3 thus imposes fixed legal obligations on the parties to an internal armed conflict to ensure humane treatment of persons not, or no longer, taking an active role in the hostilities.

Common Article 3 applies when a situation of internal armed conflict objectively exists in the territory of a State Party; it expressly binds all parties to the internal conflict, including insurgents, although they do not have the legal capacity to sign the Geneva Conventions. In Yugoslavia, the government and the UÇK forces are parties to the conflict and therefore bound by Common Article 3's provisions.

The obligation to apply Article 3 is absolute for all parties to the conflict and independent of the obligation of the other parties. That means that the Yugoslav government cannot excuse itself from complying with Article 3 on the grounds that the UÇK is violating Article 3, and vice versa.

Application of Article 3 by the government cannot be legally construed as recognition of the insurgent party's belligerence, from which recognition of additional legal obligations beyond Common Article 3, would flow. Nor is it necessary for any government to recognize the UÇK's belligerent status for Article 3 to apply.

In contrast to international conflicts, the law governing internal armed conflicts does not recognize the combatant's privilege[179] and therefore does not provide any special status for combatants, even when captured. Thus, the Yugoslav

---

[179]The "combatant's privilege" is a license to kill or capture enemy troops, destroy military objectives and cause unavoidable civilian casualties. This privilege immunizes combatants from criminal prosecution by their captors for their violent acts that do not violate the laws of war but would otherwise be crimes under domestic law. Prisoner of war status depends on and flows from this privilege. *See* Solf, "The Status of Combatants in Non-International Armed Conflicts Under Domestic Law and Transnational Practice," *American University Law Review,* No. 33 (1953), p. 59.

government is not obliged to grant captured members of the UÇK prisoner of war status. Similarly, government army combatants who are captured by the UÇK need not be accorded this status. Any party can agree to treat its captives as prisoners of war, however.

Since the UÇK forces are not privileged combatants, they may be tried and punished by the Yugoslav courts for treason, sedition, and the commission of other crimes under domestic laws.

Protocol II and the Protection of Non-combatants

Protocol II supplements Common Article 3 and provides a more encompassing list of protections for civilians in internal armed conflicts. While not an all-inclusive list, the following practices, orders, and actions are prohibited:

- Orders that there shall be no survivors, such threats to combatants, or direction to conduct hostilities on this basis.

- Acts of violence against all persons, including combatants who are captured, surrender, or are placed *hors de combat*.

- Torture, any form of corporal punishment, or other cruel treatment of persons under any circumstances.

- Pillage and destruction of civilian property. This prohibition is designed to spare civilians the suffering resulting from the destruction of their real and personal property: houses, furniture, clothing, provisions, tools, and so forth. Pillage includes organized acts as well as individual acts without the consent of the military authorities.[180]

- Hostage taking.[181]

---

[180]International Committee of the Red Cross (ICRC), *Commentary, IV Geneva Convention* (Geneva: ICRC, 1958), p.226.

[181]The ICRC *Commentary on the Additional Protocols*, p. 874, defines hostages as

persons who find themselves, willingly or unwillingly, in the power of the enemy and who answer with their freedom or their life for compliance with the orders of the latter and for upholding the security of its armed forces.

•   Desecration of corpses.[182] Mutilation of the dead is never permissible and violates the rules of war.

Protocol II also states that children should be provided with care and aid as required. Article 4, paragraph 3 states that no children under the age of fifteen shall be "recruited by the armed forces or groups."

Protection of the Civilian Population
In situations of internal armed conflict, generally speaking, a civilian is anyone who is not a member of the armed forces or of an organized armed group of a party to the conflict. Accordingly, "the civilian population comprises all persons who do not actively participate in the hostilities."[183]

Civilians may not be subject to deliberate individualized attack since they pose no immediate threat to the adversary.[184]

The term "civilian" also includes some employees of the military establishment who are not members of the armed forces but assist them.[185] While as civilians they may not be targeted, these civilian employees of military establishments or those who indirectly assist combatants assume the risk of death

---

[182]Protocol II, article 8, states:
Whenever circumstances permit, and particularly after an engagement, all possible measures shall be taken, without delay, . . . to search for the dead, prevent their being despoiled, and decently dispose of them.

[183]R. Goldman, "International Humanitarian Law and the Armed Conflicts in El Salvador and Nicaragua," *American University Journal of International Law and Policy,* Vol. 2 (1987), p. 553.

[184]M. Bothe, K. Partsch, & W. Solf, *New Rules for Victims of Armed Conflicts: Commentary on the Two 1977 Protocols Additional to the Geneva Conventions of 1949* (The Hague: Martinus Nijhoff, 1982), p. 303.

[185]Civilians include those persons who are "directly linked to the armed forces, including those who accompany the armed forces without being members thereof, such as civilian members of military aircraft crews, supply contractors, members of labour units, or of services responsible for the welfare of the armed forces, members of the crew of the merchant marine and the crews of civil aircraft employed in the transportation of military personnel, material or supplies. . . . Civilians employed in the production, distribution and storage of munitions of war. . . ." Ibid., pp. 293-94.

or injury incidental to attacks against legitimate military targets while they are at or in the immediate vicinity of military targets.

In addition, both sides may utilize as combatants persons who are otherwise engaged in civilian occupations. These civilians lose their immunity from attack for as long as they directly participate in hostilities.[186] "[D]irect participation [in hostilities] means acts of war which by their nature and purpose are likely to cause actual harm to the personnel and equipment of enemy armed forces," and includes acts of defense.[187]

"Hostilities" not only covers the time when the civilian actually makes use of a weapon but also the time that he is carrying it, as well as situations in which he undertakes hostile acts without using a weapon.[188] Examples are provided in the United States Army Field Manual which lists some hostile acts as including:

> sabotage, destruction of communication facilities, intentional misleading of troops by guides, and liberation of prisoners of war. . . . This is also the case of a person acting as a member of a weapons crew, or one providing target information for weapon systems intended for immediate use against the enemy such as artillery spotters or members of ground observer teams. [It] would include direct logistic support for units engaged directly in battle such as the delivery of ammunition to a firing position. On the other hand civilians providing only indirect support to the armed forces, such as workers in defense plants or those engaged in distribution or storage of military supplies in rear areas, do not pose an immediate threat to the adversary and therefore would not be subject to deliberate individual attack.[189]

Persons protected by Common Article 3 include members of both government and UÇK forces who surrender, are wounded, sick or unarmed, or are captured. They are *hors de combat*, literally, out of combat.

---

[186]Ibid., p. 303.

[187]ICRC, *Commentary on the Additional Protocols*, p. 619.

[188]ICRC, *Commentary on the Additional Protocols*, p. 618-19. This is a broader definition than "attacks" and includes at a minimum preparation for combat and return from combat. Bothe, *New Rules for Victims of Armed Conflicts*, p. 303.

[189]Ibid., p. 303 (footnote omitted).

Designation of Military Objectives

Under the laws of war, military objectives are defined only as they relate to objects or targets, rather than to personnel. To constitute a legitimate military objective, the object or target, selected by its nature, location, purpose, or use, must contribute effectively to the enemy's military capability or activity, and its total or partial destruction or neutralization must offer a definite military advantage in the circumstances.[190]

Legitimate military objectives are combatants' weapons, convoys, installations, and supplies. In addition:

> an object generally used for civilian purposes, such as a dwelling, a bus, a fleet of taxicabs, or a civilian airfield or railroad siding, can become a military objective if its location or use meets [the criteria in Protocol I, art. 52(2)].[191]

Full-time members of the Yugoslav government's armed forces and UÇK combatants are legitimate military targets and subject to attack, individually or collectively, until such time as they become hors de combat, that is, surrender or are wounded or captured.[192]

Policemen without combat duties are not in principle legitimate military targets, nor are certain other government personnel authorized to bear arms such as customs agents.[193] Policemen with combat duties, however, would be proper military targets, subject to direct individualized attack.

Prohibition of Indiscriminate Attacks: The Principle of Proportionality

The civilian population and individual civilians generally are to be protected against attack.

---

[190]Protocol I, art. 52 (2).

[191]Bothe, *New Rules for Victims of Armed Conflicts*, pp. 306-07.

[192]A wounded or captured combatant is "out of the fighting," and so must be protected.

[193]Report of Working Group B, Committee I, 18 March 1975 (CDDH/I/238/Rev.1; X, 93), in Howard S. Levie, ed., *The Law of Non International Armed Conflict*, (Dordrecht, Netherlands: Martinus Nijhoff, 1987), p. 67. *See* Rosario Conde, "Policemen without Combat Duties: Illegitimate Targets of Direct Attack under Humanitarian Law," student paper (New York: Columbia Law School, May 12, 1989).

As set out above, to constitute a legitimate military object, the target must 1) contribute effectively to the enemy's military capability or activity, and 2) its total or partial destruction or neutralization must offer a definite military advantage in the circumstances.

The laws of war characterize all objects as civilian unless they satisfy this two-fold test. Objects normally dedicated to civilian use, such as churches, houses and schools, are presumed not to be military objectives. If they in fact do assist the enemy's military action, they can lose their immunity from direct attack. This presumption attaches, however, only to objects that ordinarily have no significant military use or purpose. For example, this presumption would not include objects such as transportation and communications systems that under applicable criteria are military objectives.

The attacker also must do everything "feasible" to verify that the objectives to be attacked are not civilian. "Feasible" means "that which is practical or practically possible taking into account all the circumstances at the time, including those relevant to the success of military operations."[194]

Even attacks on legitimate military targets, however, are limited by the principle of proportionality. This principle places a duty on combatants to choose means of attack that avoid or minimize damage to civilians. In particular, the attacker should refrain from launching an attack if the expected civilian casualties would outweigh the importance of the military target to the attacker. The principle of proportionality is codified in Protocol I, Article 51 (5):

> Among others, the following types of attacks are to be considered as indiscriminate: . . .
>
> (b)   an attack which may be expected to cause incidental loss of civilian life, injury to civilians, damage to civilian objects, or a combination thereof, which would be excessive in relation to the concrete and direct military advantage anticipated.

If an attack can be expected to cause incidental civilian casualties or damage, two requirements must be met before that attack is launched. First, there must be an anticipated "concrete and direct" military advantage. "Direct" means "without intervening condition of agency . . . A remote advantage to be gained at

---

[194]Bothe, *New Rules for Victims of Armed Conflict*, p. 362 (footnote omitted).

some unknown time in the future would not be a proper consideration to weigh against civilian losses."[195]

Creating conditions "conducive to surrender by means of attacks which incidentally harm the civilian population"[196] is too remote and insufficiently military to qualify as a "concrete and direct" military advantage. "A military advantage can only consist in ground gained and in annihilating or weakening the enemy armed forces."[197]

The second requirement of the principle of proportionality is that the foreseeable injury to civilians and damage to civilian objects not be disproportionate, that is, "excessive" in comparison to the expected "concrete and definite military advantage."

Excessive damage is a relative concept. For instance, the presence of a soldier on leave cannot serve as a justification to destroy the entire village. If the destruction of a bridge is of paramount importance for the occupation of a strategic zone, "it is understood that some houses may be hit, but not that a whole urban area be leveled."[198] There is never a justification for excessive civilian casualties, no matter how valuable the military target.[199]

Indiscriminate attacks are defined in Protocol I, Article 51 (4), as:

a) those which are not directed at a specific military objective;
b) those which employ a method or means of combat which cannot be directed at a specific military objective; or
c) those which employ a method or means of combat the effects of which cannot be limited as required by this Protocol; and consequently, in each such case, are of a nature to strike military objectives and civilians or civilian objects without distinction.

---

[195]*Ibid.*, p. 365.

[196]ICRC, *Commentary on the Additional Protocols*, p. 685.

[197]Ibid., p. 685. As set out above, to constitute a legitimate military objective, the object, selected by its nature, location, purpose or use must contribute effectively to the enemy's military capability or activity, and its total or partial destruction or neutralization must offer a "definite" military advantage in the circumstances. See Protocol I, art. 52 (2) where this definition is codified.

[198]ICRC, *Commentary on the Additional Protocols*, p. 684.

[199]Ibid., p. 626.

The Protection of Civilians from Displacement

There are only two exceptions to the prohibition on displacement, for war-related reasons, of civilians: their security or imperative military reasons. Article 17 of Protocol II states:

> 1. The displacement of the civilian population shall not be ordered for reasons related to the conflict unless the security of the civilians involved or imperative military reasons so demand. Should such displacements have to be carried out, all possible measures shall be taken in order that the civilian population may be received under satisfactory conditions of shelter, hygiene, health, safety and nutrition.

The term "imperative military reasons" usually refers to evacuation because of imminent military operations. The provisional measure of evacuation is appropriate if an area is in danger as a result of military operations or is liable to be subjected to intense bombing. It may also be permitted when the presence of protected persons in an area hampers military operations. The prompt return of the evacuees to their homes is required as soon as hostilities in the area have ceased. The evacuating authority bears the burden of proving that its forcible relocation conforms to these conditions.

Displacement or capture of civilians solely to deny a social base to the enemy has nothing to do with the security of the civilians. Nor is it justified by "imperative military reasons," which require "the most meticulous assessment of the circumstances"[200] because such reasons are so capable of abuse. As the commentary to Protocol II states:

> Clearly, imperative military reasons cannot be justified by political motives. For example, it would be prohibited to move a population in order to exercise more effective control over a dissident ethnic group.[201]

Mass relocation or displacement of civilians for the purpose of denying a willing social base to the opposing force is prohibited as it responds to such a wholly political motive.

---

[200]Ibid., p. 1472.

[201]Ibid.

Even if the government were to show that the displacement were necessary, it still has the independent obligation to take "all possible measures" to receive the civilian population "under satisfactory conditions of shelter, hygiene, health, safety, and nutrition."

Starvation of Civilians as a Method of Combat

Starvation of civilians as a method of combat has become illegal as a matter of customary international law, as reflected in Protocol II:

> Article 14 -- Protection of objects indispensable to the survival of the civilian population
>
> Starvation of civilians as a method of combat is prohibited. It is therefore prohibited to attack, destroy, remove or render useless, for that purpose, objects indispensable to the survival of the civilian population, such as foodstuffs, agricultural areas for the production of foodstuffs, crops, livestock, drinking water installations and supplies and irrigation works.

What is prohibited is using starvation as "a weapon to annihilate or weaken the population." Using starvation as a method of warfare does not mean that the population has to reach the point of starving to death before a violation can be proved. What is forbidden is deliberately "causing the population to suffer hunger, particularly by depriving it of its sources of food or of supplies."

This prohibition on starving civilians "is a rule from which no derogation may be made."[202] No exception is allowed for imperative military necessity, for instance.

Article 14 lists the most usual ways in which starvation is brought about. Specific protection is extended to "objects indispensable to the survival of the civilian population," and a non-exhaustive list of such objects follows: "foodstuffs, agricultural areas for the production of foodstuffs, crops, livestock, drinking water installations and supplies and irrigation works." The article prohibits taking certain destructive actions aimed at these essential supplies, and describes these actions with verbs which are meant to cover all eventualities: "attack, destroy, remove or render useless."

The textual reference to "objects indispensable to the survival of the civilian population" does not distinguish between objects intended for the armed

---

[202]Ibid., p. 1456.

forces and those intended for civilians. Except for the case where supplies are specifically intended as provisions for combatants, it is prohibited to destroy or attack objects indispensable for survival, even if the adversary may benefit from them. The prohibition would be meaningless if one could invoke the argument that members of the government's armed forces or armed opposition might make use of the objects in question.[203]

Attacks on objects used "in direct support of military action" are permissible, however, even if these objects are civilian foodstuffs and other objects protected under Article 14. This exception is limited to the immediate zone of actual armed engagements, as is obvious from the examples provided of military objects used in direct support of military action: "bombarding a food-producing area to prevent the army from advancing through it, or attacking a food-storage barn which is being used by the enemy for cover or as an arms depot, etc."[204]

The provisions of Protocol I, Article 54 are also useful as a guideline to the narrowness of the permissible means and methods of attack on foodstuffs.[205] Like Article 14 of Protocol II, Article 54 of Protocol I permits attacks on military food supplies. It specifically limits such attacks to those directed at foodstuffs intended for the sole use of the enemy's armed forces. This means "supplies already in the hands of the adverse party's armed forces because it is only at that point that one could know that they are intended for use only for the members of the enemy's armed forces."[206] Even then, the attacker cannot destroy foodstuffs "in the military supply system intended for the sustenance of prisoners of war, the civilian population of occupied territory or persons classified as civilians serving with, or accompanying, the armed forces."[207]

---

[203]Ibid., p. 1458-59.

[204]Ibid., p. 657. The *New Rules* gives the following examples of direct support: "an irrigation canal used as part of a defensive position, a water tower used as an observation post, or a cornfield used as cover for the infiltration of an attacking force." Bothe, *New Rules for Victims of Armed Conflicts*, p. 341.

[205]Article 54 of Protocol I is the parallel standard, for international armed conflicts, to Article 14, Protocol II in its prohibition of starvation of civilians as a method of warfare.

[206]Bothe, *New Rules for Victims of Armed Conflict*, p. 340.

[207]Ibid., pp. 340-41.

Proof of Intent to Starve Civilians

Under Article 14, what is forbidden are actions taken with the intention of using starvation as a method or weapon to attack the civilian population. Such an intent may not be easy to prove and most armies will not admit this intent. Proof does not rest solely on the attacker's own statements, however. Intent may be inferred from the totality of the circumstances of the military campaign.

Particularly relevant to assessment of intent is the effort the attacker makes to comply with the duties to distinguish between civilians and military targets and to avoid harming civilians and the civilian economy.[208] If the attacker does not comply with these duties, and food shortages result, an intent to attack civilians by starvation may be inferred.

The more sweeping and indiscriminate the measures taken which result in food shortages, when other less restrictive means of combat are available, the more likely the real intent is to attack the civilian population by depriving it of food. For instance, an attacker who conducts a scorched earth campaign in enemy territory to deprive the enemy of sources of food may be deemed to have an intention of attacking by starvation the civilian population living in enemy territory. The attacker may not claim ignorance of the effects upon civilians of such a scorched earth campaign, since these effects are a matter of common knowledge and publicity. In particular, relief organizations, both domestic and international, usually sound the alarm of impending food shortages occurring during conflicts in order to bring pressure on the parties to permit access for food delivery and to raise money for their complex and costly operations.

The true intentions of the attacker also must be judged by the effort it makes to take prompt remedies, such as permitting relief convoys to reach the needy or itself supplying food to remedy hunger. An attacker who fails to make adequate provision for the affected civilian population, who blocks access to those who would do so, or who refuses to permit civilian evacuation in times of food shortage, may be deemed to have the intent to starve that civilian population.

Domestic Law

The federal constitution of Yugoslavia, promulgated in 1992, established Yugoslavia as a democratic state "founded on the rule of law." The forty-nine articles of the section on rights and freedoms guarantee all Yugoslav citizens basic

---

[208]Civilians are not legitimate military targets; this is also expressly established by U.N. General Assembly Resolution 2444, above. The duty to distinguish at all times between civilians and combatants, and between civilian objects and military objects, includes the duty to direct military operations only against military objectives.

civil and political rights, such as free speech, free association and the right to a fair trial.

Yugoslav laws guarantee all defendants the right to due process. Article 23 of the federal constitution forbids arbitrary detention and obliges the authorities to inform a detainee immediately of the reason for his or her detention and grant that person access to a lawyer. Article 24 obliges the authorities to inform the detainee in writing of the reason for his or her arrest within twenty-four hours. Detention ordered by a lower court may not exceed three months, unless extended by a higher court to a maximum of six months. Article 25 outlaws torture, as well as any coercion of confessions or statements. The use of force against a detainee is also a criminal offence.

The constitution guarantees the rights of minorities to "preserve, foster and express their ethnic, cultural, linguistic and other attributes, as well as to use their national symbols, in accordance with international law."[209] Article 20 states that:

> Citizens shall be equal irrespective of their nationality, race, sex, language, faith, political or other beliefs, education, social origin, property, or other personal status.

Articles 46 and 47 guarantee minorities the right to education and media in their mother tongue, as well as the right to establish educational and cultural associations. Article 48, however, places some restrictions on free association for minorities. It states:

> Members of national minorities have the right to establish and foster unhindered relations with co-nationals within the Republic of Yugoslavia and outside its borders with co-nationals in other states, and to take part in international nongovernmental organizations, *provided these relations are not detrimental to the Federal Republic of Yugoslavia or to a member republic.* [Emphasis added.]

The Yugoslav constitution also guarantees that the government will respect international law. Article 10 states:

---

[209]Constitution of the Federal Republic of Yugoslavia, Article 11.

The Federal Republic of Yugoslavia shall recognize and guarantee the rights and freedoms of man and the citizen recognized under international law.

Article 16 adds:

The Federal Republic of Yugoslavia shall fulfill in good faith the obligations contained in international treaties to which it is a contracting party. International treaties which have been ratified and promulgated in conformity with the present Constitution and generally accepted rules of international law shall be a constituent part of the internal legal order.

12. THE INTERNATIONAL WAR CRIMES TRIBUNAL FOR THE FORMER YUGOSLAVIA

The International Criminal Tribunal for the former Yugoslavia was founded in May 1993 to prosecute war crimes committed in former Yugoslavia beginning in 1991. As of September 1998, eighty individuals had been publicly indicted in connection with crimes committed in the wars in Croatia and Bosnia, while others have been the object of sealed indictments. Twenty-eight indictees were in custody, and two had been convicted of crimes, as of this writing.

Article 1 of the Tribunal's statute states that the Tribunal has the power to prosecute individuals who have committed violations of international humanitarian law on the "territory of the former Yugoslavia since 1991." Article 8 further specifies that the Tribunal's temporal jurisdiction "shall extend to a period beginning on 1 January 1991." There is no end point to this jurisdiction. Based on this mandate, violations of international humanitarian law committed in Kosovo may be investigated and prosecuted by the Tribunal.

In a March 10, 1998, press release, the prosecutor's office at the Tribunal stated publicly that the Tribunal is empowered to "prosecute persons responsible for serious violations of international humanitarian law committed in the territory of the former Yugoslavia since 1991. This jurisdiction is ongoing and covers the recent violence in Kosovo."[210] On July 7, 1998, chief prosecutor of the Tribunal, Justice Louise Arbour, wrote a letter to the Contact Group in which she reaffirmed the Tribunal's mandate and intentions in Kosovo:

> The prosecutor believes that the nature and scale of the fighting indicate that an "armed conflict", within the meaning of international law, exists in Kosovo. As a consequence, she intends to bring charges for crimes against humanity or war crimes, if evidence of such crimes is established.[211]

The Tribunal's jurisdiction includes crimes committed by armed insurgencies. In her letter to the Contact Group, Justice Arbour stressed that

---

[210]The International Criminal Tribunal for the former Yugoslavia, "Prosecutor's Statement Regarding the Tribunal's Jurisdiction Over Kosovo," The Hague, March 10, 1998.

[211]Communication from the Prosecutor to the Contact Group Members, The Hague, July 7, 1998.

"international law imposes obligations on combatants involved in an armed conflict to observe the laws of war, and any violations of such laws can be punished."

Criminal responsibility also extends to those in leadership positions if those people had reason to know that a subordinate was about to commit criminal acts, or had done so and the superior failed to take the necessary and reasonable measure to prevent such acts or to punish the perpetrators.

In early July, the Tribunal sent its first delegation to the Federal Republic of Yugoslavia regarding the Kosovo conflict. Another mission visited in September and future trips, including a high-level delegation with Chief Justice Arbour, were scheduled for later in the year. A Finnish forensics team arrived in mid-October on the invitation of the government to conduct investigations in Kosovo but, as this report went to print, it was not clear how much access the team would have and how it might cooperate with the ICTY.

On March 13, 1998, the U.S. government announced that it was providing $1.075 million to support the Tribunal's investigations in Kosovo. Since then, a number of top politicians and political bodies have publicly supported the Tribunal's work on Kosovo. On August 31, 1998, U.S. ambassador at large for war crimes issues, David Scheffer, announced that he was not able to visit Belgrade and Kosovo because he had been denied a Yugoslav visa. He told a press conference in Zagreb, Croatia:

> The United States is cooperating fully with the Tribunal as it investigates the conflict in Kosovo. We are ensuring that relevant information is provided to the Tribunal in a timely manner so that its investigations can proceed efficiently. We urge other governments to cooperate with and provide information to the War Crimes Tribunal regarding the conflict in Kosovo... .

> We strongly support the War Crimes Tribunal's intentions to fully investigate the actions in Kosovo. We trust that in the coming weeks Tribunal investigators, including forensic experts, will be given access to Kosovo and that the Tribunal will sustain a regular presence in Kosovo until the necessary investigations are completed. The Tribunal's presence on the ground in Kosovo can help deter further criminal actions as well as permit thorough examination of alleged mass grave sites and other targets of investigation. Transparency also requires secure

access by non-governmental organization which can assist in this process under the guidance of the War Crimes Tribunal.[212]

---

[212]Press conference of Ambassador David Scheffer, Zagreb, Croatia, August 31, 1998.

13. ROLE OF THE INTERNATIONAL COMMUNITY

Despite constant promises not to "repeat Bosnia," the international community has failed to take adequate steps to stop the indiscriminate targeting of civilians and the wanton destruction of their property in Kosovo. The evidence even suggests that the international community, opposed to an independent Kosovo and fearful of the UÇK's rapid growth, turned a blind eye to serious abuses by the government.

Over the past eight months, the international community has repeatedly failed to develop a unified position to resolve the conflict. Slobodan Milošević has used this divisiveness to his advantage, appearing to deal with one state, and then another, meanwhile buying himself time to advance his campaign in Kosovo. Members of the international community have taken advantage of the disunity as well: pointing to each other as the excuse for inaction.

In the instances in which the international community has sent a strong message of condemnation to the parties to the conflict, words and symbolic action have proven meaningless, with deadlines postponed, conditions abandoned, and sanctions poorly enforced and even withdrawn, notwithstanding continued violence.

The international paralysis is driven by the twin fears of endorsing Kosovo independence and of committing international resources to preserve a peaceful Kosovo within FRY. The international community is left with a policy of containment—merely guarding that the conflict does not spill over into neighboring Macedonia, Albania, and Bosnia. Human rights abuses in Kosovo have been tolerated for the sake of territorial integrity.

The October agreement with Milošević brokered by U.S. envoy Richard Holbrooke was just crystallizing as this report went to print. Most troubling was the international community's apparently firm resolve reached only after Milošević had achieved his military objectives and terrorized the Albanian population. Serious questions remain about the safety of the 2,000-person OSCE mission being sent to verify compliance, the strength of its mandate, and the international community's response should the FRY government fail to comply with U.N. Security Council resolutions 1160 and 1199.[213] (*See* Appendix D).

---

[213]The key demands of Security Council resolutions 1160 and 1199 are: a cessation of hostilities, a partial withdrawal of the security forces from Kosovo, unimpeded access for humanitarian aid agencies, cooperation with the war crimes tribunal, and the beginning of a "meaningful dialogue" between the government and the ethnic Albanian leadership on the political status of Kosovo.

Disunity within the International Community

The international response to the crisis has been considerably weakened by persistent disunity within the international community. In the Security Council, China and Russia, both permanent members with veto power, have maintained that the conflict is an internal matter for resolution by the Yugoslav authorities. This position has effectively blocked a forceful Security Council response to the conflict. Prior to September, the only measure adopted by the Security Council having any bite had been its March 31 resolution imposing an arms embargo on FRY, a position reached with China abstaining and only after repeated warnings by the Contact Group had been ignored.[214] Resolution 1199, passed on September 23 (with China abstaining again), condemned acts of violence committed in Kosovo, reaffirmed the arms embargo and, under authority of Chapter VII of the U.N. Charter, demanded an immediate cessation of hostilities. It called upon FRY and the Kosovo Albanian leadership to enter into immediate and meaningful dialogue and demanded that FRY implement immediately the measures contained in the June 12 statement of the Contact Group. The resolution called on the president of FRY to implement his own commitments from the joint statement with the president of the Russian Federation of June 16, 1998, among other things, not to carry out any repressive actions against the peaceful population, to facilitate refugee return, and to ensure full access for ICRC and UNHCR. The resolution called on the government of FRY, the Kosovo Albanian leadership, and all others to cooperate fully with the prosecutor of the ICTY, and it underlined the need for FRY authorities to bring to justice members of security forces involved in mistreatment of civilians and deliberate destruction of property. It stated that the Council would consider "further action and additional measures" if the measures demanded in its two resolutions are not taken. Porous borders and a well established Balkan arms market have kept the embargo from having any substantial impact on the ground.

A similar degree of disunity was present in the Contact Group of states dealing with matters in the Balkans—the United States, the United Kingdom, France, Germany, Italy, and Russia—where Russia in particular has again played the role of spoiler, although Russia's resistance was at times used by Western states as an excuse for their own inaction (especially those with business interests in FRY). In its first statement after the February 28 escalation of the conflict, on March 9 the Contact Group called for Security Council consideration of a comprehensive arms embargo on FRY; refusal to supply to FRY equipment that

---

[214]U.N. Security Council Resolution 1160 (1998).

might be used for internal repression or terrorism; denial of visas for senior FRY and Serbian representatives responsible for the repression; and a moratorium on government-financed export credit support for trade and investment in Serbia. Russia refused to support the last two measures, but committed to discuss additional measures if FRY failed to make progress toward fulfillment of the Contact Group's conditions. When the Contact Group met again on April 29, it noted the on-going violence and the limited progress on conditions it had previously set, and in response, the Group decided to freeze funds held abroad by the FRY and Serbian governments; and it warned if Belgrade continued to block dialogue, by May 9 the Group would impose an investment ban on Serbia. Russia refused to endorse these sanctions. At a May 9 meeting of the G-8 (the United States, Canada, the United Kingdom, France, Germany, Italy, Japan, and Russia), the gathered states agreed to implement the asset freeze and impose the investment ban, and once again Russia declared that it did not associate itself with the new sanctions.

Empty Threats of International Action

Disunity within the international community means that its statements and actions are weak, watered down to the lowest common denominator. As Slobodan Milošević knows and exploits, it also means that international condemnations, sanctions, and threats are often empty. Deadlines can be broken, conditions only partially, cynically fulfilled, and there will be only limited repercussions.

At the March 25 meeting of the Contact Group, U.S. Secretary of State Madeleine Albright warned her colleagues:

> During the Bosnian war, how many times did one party or another appear to accept our proposals, only to walk away? We say that in the former Yugoslavia, promises mean little until they are implemented with safeguards.   Incentives tend to be pocketed; warnings tend not to be believed. Leaders respond not to the distant threat of sanctions, but to the reality of sanctions.

Notwithstanding Secretary Albright's cautionary words, with which most international actors would agree, by repeatedly failing to turn the distant threat of sanctions into a reality, the international community has allowed the FRY government to make a mockery of its ultimata.

On March 9, the Contact Group gave the FRY government ten days to: withdraw the special police units and cease action by the security forces affecting the civilian population; allow access to Kosovo for the ICRC and other humanitarian organizations as well as by representatives of the Contact Group and other Embassies; commit publicly to begin a process of dialogue with the leadership of the Kosovar Albanian community; and cooperate in a constructive manner with the Contact Group. The Group proclaimed that if President Milošević took those steps, it would reconsider the sanctions imposed; if he failed to comply, they would move to further international measures, including an asset freeze on FRY and Serbian government funds abroad. Allowing ten days to slip to sixteen, the Contact Group met again on March 25. In the days prior to the March 25 meeting, the Milošević government briefly reduced the police attacks and agreed to implement an 18- month-old agreement on Albanian education rights, a long-standing demand of the international community that had been mentioned as one of many needed confidence-building measures in the March 9 Contact Group statement. Though not enough to bring the Contact Group to lift its sanctions, the FRY gestures kept the Group from imposing new sanctions and bought Milošević some time. The Contact Group agreed to meet again in four weeks to reassess the situation. To this date, Milošević has refused to pull back his special police and the education agreement, much heralded as a positive first step last March, remains to be implemented.

The Contact Group meeting of April 29 set in motion a new round of maneuvering between the international community and the FRY government. Finding that the conditions set on March 9 remained unfulfilled, the Contact Group decided to take steps to impose the asset freeze. The freeze, first promised if Belgrade did not meet Contact Group conditions by March 19, was finally endorsed by the Contact Group a month and a half later, plenty of time for the Yugoslav authorities to shelter any funds that might otherwise have been affected. The Contact Group also promised to pursue an investment ban if Milošević did not meet new conditions by May 9. Significantly, these new conditions were watered down from the March 9 ultimata, substituting a general call for "cessation of repression" for the earlier "withdraw of the special police units," and dropping the demand for access for the ICRC and humanitarian organizations altogether. As Milošević ramped up the violence, the international community lowered the bar he needed to clear to regain international acceptance.

With the asset freeze implemented and the investment ban imminent,[215] Milošević finally agreed to meet ethnic Albanian political leader Ibrahim Rugova, on May 15. The ninety minute meeting took place after five days of intense shuttle diplomacy by U.S. Special Envoy Richard Holbrooke. In a major concession to Milošević, the meeting took place without the presence of foreign mediators, a long-time condition set by both the international community and the Kosovo Albanians. Although far short of the "framework for dialogue and stabilization package" stipulated in the April 29 Contact Group statement, the international community once again eased the pressure because of the meeting. At the May 25 meeting of the European Union General Affairs Council, the foreign ministers of E.U. member states concluded that, in light of the Milošević-Rugova meeting in Belgrade, "the proposed measure to stop new investment in Serbia would not be taken forward." That week Belgrade launched a major new offensive to create a cordon sanitaire along its border with Albania that involved serious breaches of international humanitarian law. (See section on Violations in the Yugoslav-Albania Border Region.) Milošević also took some oppressive measures that affected ethnic Serbs, such as introducing a highly restrictive university law and refusing licences to some Serbian language independent media. His political ally, Momir Bulatović, was also appointed Yugoslav Prime Minister. The government offensive so soon after the meeting hurt Rugova's popularity among Albanians, but he was quickly invited for a meeting with President Clinton in Washington to bolster his public image.

The government's scorched-earth offensive, which included indiscriminate attacks on civilians and the systematic destruction of civilian property, was met with strong words but little action by the international community. Some diplomats in Kosovo told journalists that the international community was tolerating the abuses in order to force the UÇK to the negotiating table or, as one diplomat put it, to knock the UÇK "down a peg."[216] There was

---

[215]The European Union adopted a Common Position to freeze FRY and Serbian government funds on May 7, 1998. Common Position of 7 May 1998. The E.U. regulation formally imposing the asset freeze was not adopted until June 22, 1998. At a G-8 Foreign Ministers meeting on May 8-9, Canada, France, Germany, Italy, the United Kingdom, the United States, and the European Commission "agreed to implement the decision by members of the Contact Group to freeze funds held abroad by the FRY and Serbian Governments and to stop new investments in Serbia." Japan, though not joining in this action, expressed its support and willingness to study possible action. Russia refused to support the new sanctions. Conclusions of G8 Foreign Ministers, London, 8-9 May 1998.

[216]New York Times, July 29, 1998.

speculation that the West, troubled by UÇK statements that it would "liberate Priština" and form a Greater Albania, had given Milošević the green light to proceed with the offensive, as long as the conflict stayed within the borders of Kosovo.

By the June 9 meeting of E.U. foreign ministers, the pattern was getting old. The ministers finally adopted the investment ban on Serbia, together with a declaration that stated:

> President Milošević bears a special responsibility as head of the FRY government for promoting a peaceful settlement to the problems of Kosovo. He should not believe that the international community will be taken in by talk of peace when the reality on the ground is ever greater repression. . . . The European Union remains ready to press ahead with other measures against Belgrade if the authorities there fail to halt their excessive use of force and to take the steps needed for genuine political progress. Furthermore, the E.U. encourages international security organizations to pursue their efforts in this respect and to consider all options, including those which would require an authorization by the [United Nations Security Council] under Chapter VII.[217]

On June 11, NATO defense ministers directed NATO military authorities to develop a range of options for possible military action. As a demonstration of military might, they also agreed to carry out air exercises over neighboring Albania and Macedonia. These exercises, known as Operation Determined Falcon, were carried out on June 15 and heralded as a "serious message to Belgrade." Planes flew over Tirana, the Albanian capital, but not over North Albania where they would have been seen by Serbian forces and the UÇK alike.

The June 12 Contact Group meeting also reaffirmed the asset freeze and investment ban (Russia excluded) and promised additional measures unless certain steps were taken immediately. These steps were essentially the same as those that were supposed to have been implemented within ten days of March 9, except that what had once been internationally mediated dialogue and then a "framework for dialogue and a stabilization package" had become mere "rapid progress in the dialogue with the Kosovo Albanian leadership."

---

[217]Declaration by the European Union on Kosovo, Brussels, June 9, 1998.

Facing the possibility of NATO intervention, the FRY government once again looked for a bone to throw to the international community. Taking advantage of the division between Russia and the other Contact Group members, Milošević agreed to meet with Russian president Boris Yeltsin on June 16. The Milošević-Yeltsin meeting yielded Yugoslav commitments to continue talks with Kosovo Albanians, commit no repressive actions against the peaceful population, guarantee full freedom of movement on the whole territory of Kosovo, and provide unimpeded access to humanitarian organizations. Milošević also agreed to allow diplomatic observers from the United States, the European Union, and Russia, known as the Kosovo Diplomatic Observer Mission (KDOM), to monitor throughout Kosovo.

The joint statement between Milošević and Yeltsin has been honored in the breach, but it bought Milošević time at a critical juncture, when NATO intervention appeared somewhat more likely than it had at any other time up to that point.

This pattern of international engagement in the Kosovo crisis has continued to date, with many symbolic missions to the region and tough-sounding declarations, followed by little if any action. When the international community has taken action, it has either neglected to implement the measures swiftly and effectively, or it has rescinded them at the slightest concession from Milošević.

At the heart of the international community's incapacity to deal effectively with the conflict in Kosovo is its overwhelming opposition to the idea of an independent Kosovo. The international community does not want to encourage the redrawing of Yugoslav borders because of the impetus that such action might give to secessionist movements around the world and the potentially destabilizing effects an independent Kosovo might have on Bosnia and Macedonia. This is not a trivial concern. But the international community's interest in preserving international borders should not be elevated above the imperative of halting atrocities that are leading to thousands of dead and many more displaced. If the international community is to promote territorial integrity in the Balkans, it should press for the national unity that comes from respect for the rights of all citizens—a respect that has been sorely lacking in Kosovo as well as among its neighbors. But seeking to preserve Yugoslav borders by closing their eyes to the potential death of thousands is both futile and inexcusable and could lead to the regional instability that the international community is trying to avoid.

HUMAN RIGHTS WATCH

**HUMAN
RIGHTS
WATCH**

FOR IMMEDIATE RELEASE
September 29, 1998
6:00 PM (EDT)

For further information, contact:
Holly Cartner 1 (212) 216-1277

EIGHTEEN CIVILIANS MASSACRED IN KOSOVO FOREST
Thirteen Others Believed Executed

(New York, September 29, 1998) — Today Human Rights Watch reported that Serb forces massacred an extended family of eighteen ethnic Albanian civilians, including five children, in a forest in the Drenica region of Kosovo on September 26. Human Rights Watch researchers on the scene saw seven of the bodies, all of which had been shot at close range in the head. Several of the corpses had been mutilated.

"The massacre was clearly an attack on defenseless civilians who were hiding in the woods," said Holly Cartner, Executive Director of the Europe and Central Asia division of Human Rights Watch. "The Yugoslav Army and Serbian Police are fighting a war against civilians, and this is another sad example of the unspeakable atrocities being committed against them."

The Drenica region of Kosovo was considered a stronghold of the Kosova Liberation Army (UÇK), and was the sight of similar civilian massacres in February and March 1998. Human Rights Watch has seen credible evidence of similar atrocities, including the recent summary execution of thirteen men, in nearby villages.

Like thousands of ethnic Albanians in Kosovo, the Deliaj family had sought refuge in the forest after their village, Donja Obrinja, was shelled during the recent Serbian offensive. Human Rights Watch saw seven bodies located approximately 1 kilometer outside Donja Obrinja in a forested area; eleven other bodies had been carried out of the massacre site and were in the process of being buried by local villagers and other family members. The corpses of five women and two children, aged five and seven, were lying in a narrow gully near a makeshift tent where villagers said the Deliaj family had sought refuge from the shelling. All of the victims had been shot in the head at close range, apparently while attempting to flee the attack. The bodies of several of the victims displayed clear evidence of mutilation.

Luljeta Deliaj, aged twenty-eight, was two months pregnant according to family members; her belly had been cut open. According to journalists at the scene, Pajazit Deliaj, aged sixty-five, was found in the makeshift tent with his throat cut open and part of his brain removed and placed next to him. Human Rights Watch later saw photographs of Pajazit Deliaj's corpse that clearly showed that his throat had been cut and his brain mutilated.

According to one eyewitness interviewed by Human Rights Watch, the Deliaj family had been living in the forest since September 25. On September 26, at 10:00 a.m., Serbian armed forces entered the forest on foot, according to the witness, who heard shooting and screaming coming from the area of the massacre.

According to the local villagers who were burying the bodies and a count of the graves by Human Rights Watch, a total of sixteen civilians were killed in the forest. At least two other civilians were killed in the nearby village of Donja Obrinja. Several others, including two teenage girls, remain missing.

In another village, Gornja Obrinja, Human Rights Watch found the corpses of three elderly civilians, including a woman and an invalid man, who had all been shot at close range, apparently not in connection with the attack on the Doliaj family. In other villages in the area, freshly dug graves could be observed. In the village of Golubovac, located approximately five kilometers south of Donja Obrinja, Human Rights Watch visited what appeared to be the execution site of fourteen young men, whom villagers said Serbian police had beaten and executed. The site was strewn with approximately eighty spent bullet casings, and Human Rights Watch observed fresh blood stains along the fence where villagers said the men had been executed. One man reportedly survived the execution, and was interviewed by Western diplomats touring the region today.

According to eyewitnesses, police forced approximately two hundred villagers, who had been hiding in the nearby woods to escape shelling in their villages, to return to Golubovac on September 26. The eyewitnesses claimed that the police detained the group of two hundred civilians at a large house, and then selected the fourteen men for execution. One credible eyewitness told Human Rights Watch that the men were severely beaten and abused prior to execution.

The southwestern part of Drenica has been the site of a major offensive by the Yugoslav army and Serbian police over the past week. Serbian police forces have systematically burned entire villages in the region. Food supplies have been systematically destroyed. Eyewitnesses interviewed by Human Rights Watch described how they were forced to flee their villages when special police forces approached, and returned to find their homes burned and food supplies destroyed. The homes and villages inspected by Human Rights Watch often did not show any artillery or small arms marks and the evidence indicates that they were systematically burned while the villages were completely abandoned.

The targeting of civilians in war, summary executions, and the widespread destruction of civilian property constitute war crimes. Since the beginning of the Kosovo conflict in February 1998, the Yugoslav army and Serbian police have been implicated in many serious incidents of abuses against the majority ethnic Albanian population of Kosovo, suggesting a widespread disregard for the most basic principles of the laws of war and international humanitarian law.

Human Rights Watch calls on the Yugoslav authorities to respect its international obligations, and to cease all attacks on civilians and the widespread destruction of civilian objects. Further, Human Rights Watch calls on the Yugoslav authorities to provide immediate access to the area to teams of independent forensic experts to carry out investigations. The international community must take immediate steps to end abuses against civilians in Kosovo, and work to bring the perpetrators of war crimes in Kosovo to justice.

The names of the dead at Donja Obrinja are:

1) Ali Deliaj, aged sixty-three;
2) Adem Deliaj, aged thirty-three;
3) Mejhare Deliaj, aged twenty-seven and wife of Adem Deliaj;
4) Valmir Deliaj, aged eighteen months and son of Adem and Mejhare Deliaj;
5) Hamide Deliaj, aged sixty and mother of Adem Deliaj;
6) Have Deliaj, aged sixty-four or sixty-three and aunt of Adem Deliaj;
7) Lumnije Deliaj, aged thirty;
8) Jeton Deliaj, aged eight and son of Lumnije Deliaj;
9) Menduhije Deliaj, aged four and daughter of Lumnije Deliaj;
10) Luljeta Deliaj, aged twenty-eight;
11) Pajazit Deliaj, aged sixty-five;
12) Zeqir Deliaj, aged forty-four;
13) Habib Deliaj, aged fifty-three;
14) Hysen Deliaj, aged fifty-one;
15) Fazli Deliaj, aged ninety-four, invalid found dead in house;
16) Zahide Deliaj, aged twenty-seven;
17) Gentiona Deliaj, aged seven and daughter of Zahide Deliaj;
18) Donietta Deliaj, aged five and daughter of Zahide Deliaj.

Those allegedly executed in Golubovac include:

1) Remzi Veselaj, aged thirty-five, from Iglarevo;
2) Fazli Hoxhaj, aged forty-two, from Golubovac;
3) Selmon Gashi, aged thirty-one, from Plocice;
4) Rrustem Maloku, aged forty-two, from Plocice;
5) Rasim Maloku, aged thirty-eight, from Plocice;
6) Halim Maloku, aged thirty-seven, from Plocice;
7) Muhamet Maloku, aged thirty-five, from Plocice;
8) Ahmet Maloku, aged between forty-five and fifty, from Plocice;
9) Zeqir Berisha, aged forty, from Gjurgjevik;
10) Aziz Maloku, aged forty-five, from Plocice.

Three others allegedly executed in Golubovac were unidentified.

Those killed in Gornja Obrinja identified as:

1) Rrustem Hysenaj, aged seventy-three;
2) Ali Koludra, aged sixty-two, from Gremnik;
3) Hyra Koludra, aged fifty from Gremnik, wife of Ali.

FOR IMMEDIATE RELEASE

For more information, contact:
Holly Cartner 1 (212) 216-1277 in New York
Jean-Paul Marthoz (322) 736-7838 in Brussels
For photographs of the atrocities, see the website at www.hrw.org

Serb Police Attacked Convoy of 250 Vehicles
Four men killed, hundreds of men detained and abused

(New York, Wednesday, September 30, 1998)— Serbian police forces attacked a convoy of civilian vehicles and tractors on Tuesday after detaining civilians who had fled their village, Human Rights Watch reported today. A Human Rights Watch researcher saw the bodies of four ethnic Albanian men who had been killed outside Vranic, a village near Urosedac in southwestern Kosovo, including one person who was apparently executed at close range and another whose face had been mutilated.

Serbian police detained several hundred men during the attack on the convoy in Vranic. The men were then transported to the city of Prizren, where they were ill-treated in detention, according to some who were later released. Meanwhile, police burned large parts of the village of Vranic, and the shelling and burning of villages around Urosedac continued today, Human Rights Watch said.

"The Yugoslav authorities are carrying out an unrestrained campaign of terror against a civilian population," said Holly Cartner, Executive Director of the Europe and Central Asia division at Human Rights Watch. "The atrocities committed by the Serbian police and the Yugoslav army are at the core of the humanitarian crisis in Kosovo and must be stopped immediately."

Two of the four men killed were found on a hill overlooking the convoy site in Vranic and appeared to have been shot from a distance, possibly by sniper fire. Another two bodies were taken to the local mosque for burial by villagers. Miliam Bugari, age twenty-nine, had burn marks on his head that suggested he was executed at close range. Hafir Elshani, age thirty-five, was shot in the chest and his nose had been cut off.

In Vranic, Human Rights Watch saw what remained of a convoy that stretched for approximately three kilometers. Cars, tractors and trucks were loaded with civilian possessions. A Human Rights Watch eyewitness counted thirty-four vehicles in the village that had been completely destroyed and another fifty-five vehicles that had been damaged to a lesser extent. In a river valley near Vranic, Human Rights Watch saw another 145 vehicles, about half of which were destroyed or severely damaged. The possessions of civilians were strewn around the site. Many of the vehicles had been burned.

According to eyewitnesses, the inhabitants of Vranic decided to evacuate their village on

Sunday morning, September 27, after government forces began shelling the nearby villages of Bukosi and Budakovo and then began approaching the village of Vranic, where many persons from the region had sought refuge over the past two months. The civilians fled into the nearby forest above Vranic, where they spent Sunday night.

Eyewitnesses told Human Rights Watch that the convoy was approached by an elderly man Monday morning who conveyed a message from the police that it was safe for them to return home. The convoy began returning to Vranic, but the first part of the convoy was stopped by police in the center of the village. Police then began screening all the civilians in the convoy. Witnesses told Human Rights Watch that women and children were detained in a school compound in Vranic while the men were separated into two groups, one detained in a large house in Vranic and another taken to a school in nearby Bukosi. While the civilians were kept in detention, police started to burn houses in Vranic and destroy many of the cars in the convoy.

According to eyewitnesses, the estimated 250 to 300 men detained in the house in Vranic were transferred to a fire station adjoining the police station in Prizren on Monday afternoon or Tuesday morning. Most were returned by police to Vranic around 3:00 p.m. today while Human Rights Watch was on the scene. The men detained in Bukosi were also released.

The men who were returned from custody in Prizren told Human Rights Watch that they had been beaten by police with fists and rubber batons. They showed injuries that were consistent with their accounts, including swollen hands and bruises on the body. They also reported that they had not received any food or water since being detained. According to the released persons, approximately fifty people from the Vranic convoy remain in detention in Prizren.

While approaching the town of Vranic, Human Rights Watch saw the village of Budakovo burning in the background. According to local villagers and international monitors interviewed by Human Rights Watch, Budakovo was shelled on the morning of September 30 before police moved in to burn homes in the town.
Also on September 30, members of the International Committee of the Red Cross (ICRC) hit a landmine on a road outside of Libovac, injuring three ICRC staff and killing an ethnic Albanian doctor, Dr. Shpetim Robaj. Several other anti-tank mines were removed today from the area, which was also the location of two earlier mine explosions, one involving the Canadian-Kosovo Diplomatic Observer Mission (KDOM) team and one that killed five Serbian policemen. Human Rights Watch called upon all parties to the conflict to refrain from the use of land mines.

Human Rights Watch urges the government of Yugoslavia to end all attacks on civilians immediately and to stop the widespread destruction of civilian property. In light of widespread and continuing evidence of torture and physical abuse in detention and at least five documented deaths in police custody in the past two months due to physical abuse, Human Rights Watch is particularly concerned about the treatment of those from Vranic who are currently detained in Prizren and calls upon the government of Yugoslavia to treat persons in custody humanely. Human Rights Watch also calls upon the government of Yugoslavia to allow international monitors such as the ICRC and human rights groups to have immediate and unconditional access to all detainees to monitor their treatment is custody.

HUMAN RIGHTS WATCH
350 Fifth Avenue, 34th Floor
New York, NY 10118-3299
Telephone: (212) 290-4700
Facsimile: (212) 736-1300
E-mail: hrwnyc@hrw.org

Website: http://www.hrw.org
EUROPE AND CENTRAL ASIA DIVISION
Holly Cartner
Executive Director
Rachel Denber
Deputy Director
Elizabeth Andersen
Advocacy Director
Diederik Lohmann
Moscow Office Director
Pamela Gomez
Caucasus Office Director
Fred Abrahams
Julia Hall
Malcolm Hawkes
Andreas Lommen
Christopher Panico
Diane Paul
Marie Struthers
Research Associates
Alexander Petrov
Assistant Moscow Office Director
Acacia Shields
Coordinator
Caucasus/Central Asia
Liudmila Belova
Alex Frangos
Joshua Sherwin
Associates
STEERING COMMITTEE
Peter Osnos, *Chair*
Alice H. Henkin, *Vice Chair*
Morton Abramowitz
Barbara Finberg
Frederica Friedman
Felice Gaer
Michael Gellert
Paul Goble
Bill Green
Stanley Hoffmann
Robert James
Kati Marton
Prema Mathai-Davis
Jack Matlock
Karl Meyer
Joel Motley
Herbert Okun
Jane Olson
Barnett Rubin
Leon Sigal
Malcolm Smith
George Soros
Donald J. Sutherland
Ruti Teitel
Mark Walton
William D. Zabel
Warren Zimmermann
HUMAN RIGHTS WATCH
Kenneth Roth
Executive Director
Michele Alexander
Development Director
Carroll Bogert
Communications Director
Reed Brody
Advocacy Director
Cynthia Brown
Program Director
Barbara Guglielmo
Finance & Administration Director
Susan Osnos
Associate Director
Wilder Tayler
General Counsel
Lotte Leicht
Brussels Office Director
Joanna Weschler
United Nations Representative
Jonathan Fanton
Chair

APPENDIX C

FOR IMMEDIATE RELEASE

For more information, contact:
Holly Cartner 1 (212) 216-1277 in New York
Jean-Paul Marthoz (322) 736-7838 in Brussels

Human Rights Watch Interviews Sole Survivor of Golubovac Execution of Thirteen, Expresses Concern for His Safety

(New York Thursday, October 1, 1998) Human Rights Watch today interviewed the sole survivor of a September 26 summary execution of thirteen men by Serbian police. The witness gave a coherent and credible account of the summary execution which was corroborated by the evidence found at the execution site and the testimony of another witness interviewed by Human Rights Watch on September 29.

Human Rights Watch expressed serious concern today about the safety of the survivor in light of the Serbian police presence in the region, and called upon the international community to take the necessary steps to relocate this important witness to a safe location. Furthermore, the man has a severe and infected gunshot wound on his upper left leg, as well as gunshot wounds on his left arm, and is in need of immediate medical attention. "The survivor is a credible witness to a summary execution, and the ability to bring the perpetrators of this serious war crime to justice hinges on his safety," said Holly Cartner. "The international community must take immediate steps to insure that he is safe and his testimony is preserved."

During an interview today, he told Human Rights Watch that the inhabitants of his village Golubovac in the Drenica region of Kosovo had fled into the nearby forest on Friday morning after Yugoslav forces began shelling around the neighboring village of Cerovik. The villagers spent the night in the forest.

According to the survivor, Serb police sent several elderly ethnic Albanian villagers who had remained in Golubovac to the forest on Saturday morning to tell the civilians taking shelter there that it was safe for them to return home. When they attempted to return, they were then gathered in a field by a group of about thirty or forty police officers, and the men were separated from the women and children. The police initially chose about twenty-five men from the larger group of men, but then narrowed this group down to fourteen men who, according to the survivor, would later be lined up and shot.

The survivor told Human Rights Watch that the fourteen were beaten with fists and rifles and kicked with boots while being questioned by Serb police about ties to the Kosovo Liberation Army (UÇK). The process of separating the men and their subsequent interrogation lasted for about two hours. The men were then taken to the road next to the execution site, where they were forced to crouch with their hands behind their backs for an extended period of time.

The survivor told Human Rights Watch that the men were then led into a garden and ordered to lie flat on the ground, face down with their hands behind their backs. They were told that if they identified UÇK members in their midst everyone else would be freed. During this time, the survivor reported being beaten on his back with sticks and kicked all over his body. He showed Human Rights Watch deep bruises on his back and buttocks that were consistent with this account. He also described in detail how the men were executed, relating how a single police officer first executed the man lying next to the survivor and then two other men nearby. The police officer then moved up and down the column firing a burst of automatic gunshots at each victim. Several of the men were kicked afterwards and one man was shot again when he displayed signs of life. The witness apparently survived because he was able to feign death when being kicked. The police left the site almost immediately after the execution and the survivor was helped from the scene by local villagers.

The testimony of the survivor was coherent and credible, and matched the testimony of an earlier witness previously interviewed by Human Rights Watch, as well as the evidence inspected at the execution site on Tuesday. Along a fence within a family compound, Human Rights Watch inspected many pools of fresh blood on Tuesday and found over eighty bullet shells at the spot where the witnesses claimed the policeman fired. The site was also visited by diplomatic observers on Tuesday.

Human Rights Watch is greatly concerned about the health and safety of the sole survivor, who remains in the Drenica region, which is under heavy Serbian police control. Human Rights Watch calls upon the international community to assist the International Criminal Tribunal for the Former Yugoslavia (ICTY) in bringing the survivor to a safe location, and demands that the Yugoslav authorities and police and military forces refrain from any actions that would jeopardize the safety of this important witness.

The violations of humanitarian law being committed in Kosovo fall under the jurisdiction of the ICTY. By taking immediate steps to collect and preserve evidence and witnesses' testimony, the Tribunal will not only increase the chances of ultimately bringing the perpetrators to justice, but also of deterring future abuses. However, time is of the essence if the tribunal is to fulfill its enormous deterrence potential. Much more intense and timely attention to ongoing atrocities are required.

In order for the ICTY to meet this challenge, it must have sufficient capacity and equipment on site to conduct an immediate investigation when allegations of atrocities emerge. Further, its investigators, including forensic experts, must have unimpeded access to the sites of recent abuses. To date, the Yugoslav government has denied entry visas to forensic teams, investigators of the ICTY, and other respected and impartial international organizations in a blatant attempt to prevent international and independent scrutiny of the abuses committed by its forces. Human Rights Watch calls upon the international community to assist the ICTY in developing such urgently needed capacities, and on the Yugoslav government to provide immediate access for the ICTY and its independent forensic experts to carry out investigations into allegations of mass graves and other atrocities in the region.

HUMAN RIGHTS WATCH

350 Fifth Avenue, 34th Floor
New York, NY 10118-3299
Telephone: 212-2904700
Facsimile: 212-736-1300

Website: http://www.hrw.org
**EUROPE AND CENTRAL ASIA
DIVISION**
Holly Cartner
Executive Director
Rachel Denber
Deputy Director
Elizabeth Andersen
Advocacy Director
Diederik Lohmann
Moscow Office Director
Pamela Gomez
Caucasus Office Director
Fred Abrahams
Julia Hall
Malcolm Hawkes
Andreas Lommen
Christopher Panico
Diane Paul
Marie Struthers
Research Associates
Alexander Petrov
Assistant Moscow Office Director
Acacia Shields
Coordinator
Caucasus/Central Asia
Liudmila Belova
Alex Frangos
Joshua Sherwin
Associates
STEERING COMMITTEE
Peter Osnos, *Chair*
Alice H. Henkin, *Vice Chair*
Morton Abramowitz
Barbara Finberg
Frederica Friedman
Felice Gaer
Michael Gellert
Paul Goble
Bill Green
Stanley Hoffmann
Robert James
Kati Marton
Prema Mathai-Davis
Jack Matlock
Karl Meyer
Joel Motley
Herbert Okun
Jane Olson
Barnett Rubin
Leon Sigal
Malcolm Smith
George Soros
Donald J. Sutherland
Ruti Teitel
Mark Walton
William D. Zabel
Warren Zimmermann
HUMAN RIGHTS WATCH
Kenneth Roth
Executive Director
Michele Alexander
Development Director
Carroll Bogert
Communications Director
Reed Brody
Advocacy Director
Cynthia Brown
Program Director
Barbara Guglielmo
*Finance & Administration
   Director*
Susan Osnos
Associate Director
Wilder Tayler
General Counsel
Lotte Leicht
Brussels Office Director
Joanna Weschler
*United Nations
   Representative*
Jonathan Fanton

APPENDIX D

October 20, 1998

Human Rights Watch Recommendations on theOSCE Kosovo Verification Mission

In light of the Federal Republic of Yugoslavia's (FRY) poor record of cooperation with the international community, Human Rights Watch is concerned that the OSCE Kosovo Verification Mission, established to monitor compliance with Security Council Resolutions 1160 and 1199, may face serious incidents of non-compliance and obstruction of its work.

It is critically important therefore, that the international community establish clear benchmarks toward which substantial progress must be made before the OSCE mission is deployed—expending OSCE political capital and putting a substantial number of unarmed civilian personnel at risk. It is also essential that once deployed, the mission has a strong, pro-active human rights orientation. This briefing paper details Human Rights Watch's specific recommendations regarding necessary pre-deployment compliance and the human rights activities of the mission.

Pre-deployment Benchmarks:
The recent history of peace-making in the Balkans has been a story of broken promises. Since the conflict in Kosovo broke out last February, the government of Slobodan Milosevic has repeatedly promised compliance with international demands, only promptly to renege and renew its abusive campaign against the Kosovo Albanians. The current failure of Milosevic to make promised troop withdrawals—causing NATO to extend its deadline for compliance from October 17 to October 27—is a worrisome sign that the pattern may continue. Equally troubling is evidence that the KLA has broken its ceasefire.

By pursuing their mandate aggressively and publicly, the proposed OSCE monitors may help create an environment in which civilians feel less at risk. But as unarmed civilians, with their authority ultimately limited to verification, the OSCE personnel may be powerless to stop abuses and may even become targets themselves.

Before the OSCE puts its imprimatur on the peace process and its personnel at risk, it must insist on several key indicators of FRY's good faith implementation of its commitments. The existing Kosovo Diplomatic Observer Mission (KDOM) is well placed to provide this interim verification. *Human Rights Watch believes that, at a minimum, the OSCE should receive clear indication of substantial progress toward fulfillment of the following important benchmarks prior to the deployment:*

- *Withdrawal of all Serbian special police forces and any paramilitary units that have or are suspected of having perpetrated human rights or humanitarian law violations in Kosovo; and disclosure of information regarding the command structure for all remaining forces, including the identities and locations of all commanding officers.*

- *Guaranteed safe passage and unincumbered access for humanitarian aid delivery and distribution to displaced persons throughout Kosovo.*

- *Full cooperation with the Prosecutor of the International Criminal Tribunal for the former Yugoslavia in her investigation into alleged atrocities committed in Kosovo, including the provision of unrestricted access to the territory and full investigatory rights.*

- *Disclosure of all current places of detention where persons detained in connection with the conflict are being held; disclosure of the names of all individuals detained during the course of the conflict and their current whereabouts; and provision of full and unfettered access for humanitarian organizations to all detainees, including those who are currently being investigated but have not been charged with a crime.*

Only upon compliance with these minimum requirements for a lasting peace can the OSCE verification mission hope to be successfully deployed.

The Mandate of the Verification Mission:

Human Rights Watch believes that the OSCE mission must maintain a strong human rights orientation for its work. The U.N.'s conclusions in a recent non-paper on lessons learned from the UNTAES mission to Croatia are instructive:

- In Eastern Slavonia, the establishment of a safe and secure environment was essential to the return of refugees and displaced persons.

- The monitoring of human rights was closely associated with the return of refugees and displaced persons. As the level of respect for human rights rose, so did the rate of return of refugees and displaced persons.

*   *   *

- The constant presence of CIVPOL in all police stations provided an essential reassurance to local residents that their basic human rights would be protected during criminal investigations and when in police custody.

- OSCE and ECMM together with CIVPOL worked closely in monitoring human rights, thereby demonstrating the consensus in the international community on the importance of respect for human rights.

- It was essential for the future of the region to improve the professionalism and knowledge of the region's TPF in the field of human rights by providing on-site training, special courses on identification of, investigation and reporting on, human rights violations.[218]

Similarly, in Kosovo, the humanitarian crisis that has driven recent peacemaking efforts can only be solved if the Verification Mission effectively addresses the human rights violations that caused the crisis in the first place. To do so, the mission must be authorized and obliged to investigate and monitor ongoing human rights and humanitarian law violations, collect information on past abuses, cooperate with international organizations, including the International Criminal Tribunal for the former Yugoslavia, and regularly publicize its activities and findings. These activities have been implicitly agreed in the October 16 agreement between the Yugoslav authorities and the OSCE, as they are essential to fulfillment of the Mission's mandate to, inter alia, facilitate the return of displaced persons, monitor the conduct of the police, and facilitate ICRC access to detainees.

Drawing from our experience in other peace-keeping and -implementing missions throughout the world, Human Rights Watch believes that the human rights responsibilities of the mission should be coordinated by a specialized unit, well-staffed by persons with the necessary expertise and operating under the direct supervision of the head of mission. All members of the OSCE mission should receive training in human rights monitoring and the mission should include staff with field experience in monitoring human rights abuses and interviewing victims and witnesses of atrocities, including torture, rape, and sexual abuse; forensic experts; legal experts knowledgeable in international human rights and humanitarian law; specialists in police and military methodology; and those knowledgeable in building civil society and democratic institutions. The Mission's periodic reports to the Security Council and Permanent Council should contain a specific section devoted to human rights-related developments, and these findings and recommendations should be publicly available.

---

[218] Non-Paper, "Lessons Learned from the United Nations Transitional Administration in Eastern Slavonia, Baranja and Western Sirmium (UNTAES) and Cooperation Between the United Nations and the North Atlantic Treaty Organization (NATO) and the Organization for Security and Cooperation in Europe," p.30, May 1998.

The human rights mandate of the mission should be clearly set forth in a mission statement of the OSCE prior to the deployment of its monitors. Specifically, the human rights mandate of the OSCE mission should empower and oblige the mission to:

Freely monitor and investigate human rights conditions:
- Receive complaints of human rights abuses from any person or group in Kosovo.

- Travel freely and visit any site, including any suspected or known places of detention.

- Interview persons freely and in private, including detainees who have not yet been charged with a crime.

Monitor, report, and publicize abuses committed by the security forces:
- Monitor the behavior of the Serbian police and Yugoslav Army and investigate incidents of harassment or violence against the population; raise cases of abuse with the appropriate authorities; recommend corrective action, including dismissal or prosecution; and publicize the abuses, particularly in cases where the authorities fail to take appropriate corrective action.

Monitor, report, and publicize KLA abuses:
- Monitor and investigate any harassment or abuse by the Kosovo Liberation Army against ethnic Albanians, Serbs, and others; report those abuses to the KLA and the Yugoslav authorities; recommend accountability or other corrective action in conformity with international standards; and publicize the abuses, particularly where the KLA or Yugoslav authorities fail to take appropriate corrective action.

Monitor, report, and publicize conditions of detention:
- In cooperation with ICRC, monitor the treatment of those in detention through regular visits to prisons and police stations and suspected places of detention, including those located outside of Kosovo but holding persons detained in connection with the conflict; interview detainees, freely and in private, including those who have not yet been charged with a crime; raise objections with the authorities when access to detention facilities is denied or conditions deviate from international standards; recommend corrective action, including dismissal or prosecution; and publicize those conditions when the authorities fail to take corrective action, including the prosecution of responsible officials.

Monitor, report, and publicize conduct of trials:
- Observe trials, especially those of ethnic Albanians accused of "terrorism" or other crimes related to state security; raise objections with the authorities when access to trials is denied and when procedural irregularities are identified; recommend remedial measures; and publicize procedural violations, particularly when the authorities fail to take remedial action.

Monitor, report, and publicize conditions for return of displaced persons:

- Monitor and investigate obstacles to the right of return for the estimated 250,000 internally displaced persons in Kosovo; bring those obstacles to the attention of the authorities; recommend remedial measures; and publicize the problem, particularly when the authorities fail to remedy it.

Monitor, report, and publicize restrictions on the media:
- Monitor and investigate restrictions on freedom of the press in Serbia, both on the Albanian- and Serbian-language media; publicize deficiencies in freedom of expression and recommend needed reform to the authorities.

Work with local and international human rights organizations:
- Maintain close contact with local and international human rights organizations working in Kosovo and develop procedures for regular consultation and information sharing.

Cooperate with the ICTY:
- Cooperate fully with the International Criminal Tribunal for the Former Yugoslavia by identifying possible witnesses and evidence of violations of international humanitarian law. To facilitate this cooperation, Mission members should be briefed on the specific evidentiary needs of the ICTY and instructed to forward relevant information.

Contribute to human rights institution building:
- Lead or participate in efforts to assist in the development of national institutions—both governmental and nongovernmental—which can protect and promote human rights after the international monitoring has ended.

Vet the police force for human right abusers:
- As part of police force development envisioned by the agreement, ensure that all police officers responsible for war crimes or other serious human rights violations are not allowed to serve in any capacity in law enforcement. For purposes of the vetting of police officers, the OSCE should seek information regarding individual police officers' human rights record from the ICTY, local and international human rights groups, the public, as well as from the OSCE's own human rights monitors.

In conclusion, Human Rights Watch notes that the OSCE should not limit its engagement in FRY to the verification mission. First, the new OSCE mission to Kosovo should not be considered a replacement for the long-term, Yugoslav-wide OSCE mission that was expelled from the country in 1992. Such a mission to monitor human rights conditions throughout Yugoslavia is essential to any viable long-term political solution in FRY and should remain a central demand of the international community. Second, recognizing limitations on his mandate, Human Rights Watch believes that the OSCE High Commissioner on National Minorities might play an important role in Kosovo, providing an early warning mechanism for possible renewed violence stemming from abuses committed against Albanians, Serbs or other minorities resident in the region. Finally, the OSCE should support recent efforts of its Representative on Freedom of the Media to address the serious violations of free expression that undermine prospects for any lasting political solution in FRY.